ALL THE SULTAN'S MEN

The *ulema* having a feast with the Sultan (circa 1720)
Source: *Surname-ı Sultan Ahmed Han*.
Topkapı Sarayı Müzesi, Istanbul (Inv.3593/49b).

مَا رَوَاهُ الْأَسَاطِينُ فِي عَدَمِ الْمَجِيءِ إِلَى السَّلَاطِينَ

ALL THE SULTAN'S MEN

Being a Translation of Imam Jalal al-Din al-Suyuti's
ma rawahu al-asatin fi 'adam al-maji' ila al-salatin

By the Polymath Mujtahid
JALAL AL-DIN AL-SUYUTI

Translation
TALUT DAWOOD

Imam Ghazali
INSTITUTE

© 2021 IMAM GHAZALI INSTITUTE
No part of this publication may be reproduced, stored in a retrieval
system, or transmitted in any form or by any means, electronic
or otherwise, including photocopying, recording, and internet
without prior permission of the IMAM GHAZALI INSTITUTE.

Title: ALL THE SULTAN'S MEN
ISBN: 978-1-952306-07-5

FIRST EDITION

Author: JALAL AL-DIN AL-SUYUTI
Translator: TALUT DAWOOD
Proofreaders: WORDSMITH
Typeset: IDRIS KAMAL

IMAM GHAZALI INSTITUTE
info@imamghazali.org | www.imamghazali.org

The views, information, or opinions expressed are solely those of the author(s) and do not
necessarily represent those of Imam Ghazali Institute.

CONTENTS

	TRANSLATOR'S INTRODUCTION	9
	AL-SUYUTI ﷺ BY SHAYKH DR GIBRIL HADDAD	11

ALL THE SULTAN'S MEN

1.	THE PROHIBITION OF VISITING THE RULERS IN THE PROPHETIC SUNNAH	31
2.	THE MOST HATED OF PEOPLE TO ALLAH ﷻ	32
3.	WILL THE PERSON WHO ENTERS UPON THE RULER DRINK FROM THE LAKE OF THE PROPHET ﷺ?	34
4.	THE JURISTS ARE THE CUSTODIANS OF THE MESSENGERS	36
5.	THE SCHOLAR WILL HAVE THE SAME PUNISHMENT AS THE RULER	37
6.	FROM THE ATTRIBUTES OF THE SCHOLARS OF THE END TIMES	38
7.	SEDITIOUS RULERS	40
8.	PEOPLE WHO WILL STUDY THE JURISPRUDENCE OF THE RELIGION FOR THE GOODS OF THIS WORLD	41
9.	THE RULING OF ONE WHO APPROACHES THE RULER THROUGH FLATTERY	42
10.	WARNING AGAINST SITTING IN THE RULER'S GATHERING	44
11.	THE ONE WHO VISITS THE RULER LOSES HIS RELIGION	45
12.	BLAMEWORTHY TRAITS IN THE SEEKERS OF KNOWLEDGE	46
13.	BEWARE OF GOING HEADLONG INTO SEDITION	47
14.	THE COUNSEL OF WAHB IBN MUNABBIH TO 'ATA'	48
15.	DO NOT SIT WITH HERETICAL PEOPLE	49
16.	BEWARE OF DESIRES AND DISPUTES	50
17.	THE STATES OF THE PIOUS PREDECESSORS REGARDING THE GOVERNORS	52
18.	THREE KINDS OF SCHOLARS	55
19.	THE BENEFIT OF THE PEOPLE OF KNOWLEDGE DEFENDING KNOWLEDGE	57
20.	ABU HAZIM AL-ZAHID AND THE RULERS OF BANI UMAYYAH	59
21.	HAMMAD IBN SALAMAH AND THE GOVERNOR OF IRAQ	63
22.	THE SITUATION OF THOSE WHO ASSOCIATE WITH THE RULERS	65
23.	THAT WHICH IS UNBECOMING OF THE SCHOLAR	71
24.	THE MOST NOBLE THING IN THE END TIMES	75
25.	THE WORDS OF SOME POETS ON COMING TO THE RULERS	76

"I don't fear them debasing or disgracing me. Rather, I fear them being generous towards me so that my heart inclines towards them."

SUFYAN AL-THAWRI

Translator's Introduction

THE DECISION TO TRANSLATE THIS WORK by the great polymath and *mujtahid* Imam Jalal al-Din al-Suyuti comes in a timely fashion and specific context. The times we live in are confusing and often difficult to understand. In recent years, political engagement has taken up much attention in the minds, resources, and activities of Muslims in the West. Our faith is holistic, but ultimately, as Muslims our understanding of this topic is within the confines of sacred parameters.

Since the age of early Muslims when the Prophetic *Khilafah* ended and the era of Muslim kings and empires began, scholars have wrestled with the nature of the relationship between the ulema-class and rulers. Some of our most illustrious Imams, such as Imam Abu Hanifah and Imam Malik, refused official appointments from rulers. Moreover, they refused to visit them in their courts. The rulers were made to visit their circles of knowledge if they wished to speak with them. Others such as Qadi Abu Yusuf—the student of Imam Abu Hanifah—accepted official appointments. Such disparity in the way of dealing with the rulers was echoed throughout the time of the *tabi'in*. Some scholars accepted appointments, while others criticized them and refused such an association.

In many ways, the scholarly circles of our time are no different. Some scholars have accepted appointments in an attempt to provide as much good as possible by giving counsel to rulers. Others, on the other hand, have steered clear from such controversial opinions, believing it to be best for their religion and the religion of their followers. Each party has its evidence and has exercised its *ijtihad* given the current circumstances.

Nonetheless, both scholar and layman require guidance on the correct measures to take in times of confusion. One may wonder,

"*When is it acceptable for a scholar to accept an appointment?*" Or "*When is it appropriate for a scholar to avoid politics altogether?*" Others may ask, "*Is there a middle ground between the two opinions?*" Such questions require in-depth answers. Although this text is only an introduction to the subject, it provides clear guidance on what kinds of interactions with the rulers are blameworthy for scholars, and why.

ALL THE SULTAN'S MEN is a translation of Imam al-Suyuti's text *ma rawahu al-asatin fi 'adami al-maji'i ila al-salatin*. As indicated by the title, it argues and establishes the blameworthy nature of scholars associating with rulers.

Such a relationship is considered blameworthy because it places the scholar in a precarious position. If he receives favour in the ruler's court, then it may lead him to be silent in the face of oppression, or it may give the ruler influence over him and his religious rulings. These are from the seditions and afflictions that must be avoided for the sake of Allah and His Religion. Otherwise, the scholar will tread the path of one who does not benefit from his knowledge nor benefits anyone else. Furthermore, the Hadiths and sayings of the righteous regarding such a person are of course well-known.

By masterfully interweaving Prophetic traditions and reports on the early Muslim Scholars, al-Suyuti creates a roadmap for those that follow. He first establishes that it is not permitted for a scholar to visit the ruler. He explains why, and then provides examples of situations when this impermissibility is lifted. Both scholars and ordinary Muslim worshipers will come away with an understanding of the proper etiquette of dealing with a ruler or government. They will also be encouraged to do as much as possible to refrain from being involved with oppressive governments and rulers in order to safeguard their Hereafter.

May Allah give us the ability to identify evil as evil and stay far from it. May He grant us success in all our affairs and allow us to stay true to the Muhammadan way.

TALUT DAWOOD
15 JUMADA AL-ULA 1442 | 30 DECEMBER 2020

AL-SUYUTI
B. 849AH | D. 911AH

ABD AL-RAHMAN B. KAMAL AL-DIN Abi Bakr b. Muhammad b. Sabiq al-Din Jalal al-Din al-Misri al-Suyuti al-Shafi'i al-Ash'ari (849-911), also known as Ibn al-Suyuti, was a *mujtahid imam* and reformer of the tenth Islamic century. He was a prominent Hadith Master, jurist, Sufi, philologist and historian, who authored works in virtually every Islamic science.

Born to a Turkish mother and a father of Persian origin, he was raised as an orphan in Cairo. He memorized the Qur'an at the age of eight, followed by several complete works of Sacred Law, fundamentals of jurisprudence, and Arabic grammar. He then devoted his life to studying the Sacred Sciences under approximately 150 sheikhs. Among them were the foremost Shafi'i and Hanafi sheikhs at the time, such as *Sheikh al-Islam* Siraj al-Din al-Bulqini, with whom he studied Shafi'i jurisprudence; the Hadith scholar *Sheikh al-Islam* Sharaf al-Din al-Munawi, with whom he read Qur'anic exegesis and who commented on al-Suyuti's *al-jami' al-saghir* in a book entitled *fayd al-qadir*; and Taqi al-Din al-Shamani, with whom he studied Hadith and the sciences of Arabic. Al-Suyuti also studied with Jalal al-Din al-Mahalli, a specialist in the principles of the law, together with whom he compiled the most widespread, condensed commentary on the Qur'an of our time: *tafsir al-jalalayn*. Some Hanafi sheikhs he studied under include Shihab al-Din al-Sharmisahi, Muhyi al-Din al-Kafayji, and the Hadith Master Sayf al-Din Qasim b. Qatlubagha.

In the pursuit of knowledge, al-Suyuti travelled to Damascus, the Hejaz, Yemen, India and Morocco, as well as to centers of learning in Egypt such as Mahalla, Dumyat, and Fayyum. He spent some time as the head teacher of Hadith at the Shaykhuniyya school in Cairo, at the recommendation of Imam Kamal al-Din b. al-Humam. He then took up the same position at Baybarsiyya, but was dismissed due to complaints from other sheikhs whom he had replaced. After this, he retired into scholarly seclusion and did not return to the field of teaching.

Ibn Iyas, in *tarikh misr*, reveals that when al-Suyuti reached forty years of age, he abandoned the company of men for the solitude of the garden of al-Miqyas, by the side of the river Nile, where he avoided his former colleagues as though he had never known them. It was there that he authored the majority of his nearly 600 books and treatises. Wealthy Muslims and princes would visit him with offers of money and gifts but he rejected them and also refused the Sultan many times when he requested al-Suyuti s presence. He once said to the Sultan's envoy: '*Do not ever come back to us with a gift, for in truth Allah has put an end to all such needs for us.*'

He was blessed with great success in his years of solitude making it difficult to name a field in which al-Suyuti did not make outstanding contributions. Among his most prominent works is his ten-volume Hadith collection *jam' al-jawami'* ('The Collection of Collections'); his Qur'anic exegesis *tafsir al-jalalayn* ('Commentary of the Two Jalals') in which he finished the second half of an uncompleted manuscript by Jalal al-Din Mahalli in just forty days; and his classic commentary on the sciences of Hadith *tadrib al-rawi fi sharh taqrib al-nawawi* ('The Training of the Hadith Transmitter: An Exegesis of Nawawi's "The Facilitation"').

A giant among contemporary scholars, he produced a sustained output of scholarly writings until his death at the age of sixty two. He was buried in Hawsh Qawsun in Cairo. In the introduction to his book entitled *al-riyad al-aniqa* on the names of the Prophet 🕌 he said: '*It is my hope that Allah accepts this book and that through this book I shall gain the intercession of the Prophet 🕌. Perhaps it shall be that Allah makes it the seal of all my works, and grants me what I have asked Him with longing, regarding the Honorable One.*'

The editors of *dalil makhtutat al-suyuti* ('Guide to al-Suyuti's Manuscripts') have listed 723 works to his name.[1] Some of these are brief *fatawa* which do not exceed four pages, such as his notes on the hadith '*Whoever says: "I am knowledgeable" he is ignorant*' entitled *a'dhab al-manahil fi hadith man qala ana 'alim*. Other works of his, for instance *itqan fi 'ulum al-qur'an* and *tadrib al-rawi*, are complete tomes.

Al-Tabarani stated that the above hadith is only narrated through the chain containing al-Layth b. Abi Sulaym, which is a weak chain. Al-'Ajluni in *kashf al-khafa'* says that this hadith is narrated by al-Tabarani in *al-Awsat* from Ibn 'Umar, rather than the Prophet ﷺ. Al-Haytami states in *al-fatawa al-hadithiyya* that this is simply a saying of the *tabi'i* Yahya b. Kathir. For his part, Ibn Kathir cites it from 'Umar in his tafsir of the verse: '*Have you not seen those who praise themselves for purity?*' (al-Nisa' 4: 49).Three narrations regarding this hadith are mentioned from 'Umar in *kanz al-'ummal*, but all of them are weak.

Al-'Iraqi in his *al-Mughni* explains that the part actually attributed to Yahya b. Kathir is: '*Whoever says: "I am a believer", he is a disbeliever*' while al-Haythami in *majma' al-zawa'id* cites from Ibn Kathir, with a weak chain, as follows: '*Whoever says: "I am knowledgeable", he is ignorant, and whoever says: "I am ignorant", he is ignorant. Whoever says: "I am in Paradise", he is in the Fire, and whoever says: "I am in the Fire", he is in the Fire.*' Al-Haythami further added: '*It is established from countless Companions and others that they said they were knowledgeable, and they would not do anything which the Prophet ﷺ had criticized. A greater proof is Yusuf's statement: "I am a knowledgeable guardian"*' (Yusuf 12: 55).

However, the narration of al-Layth is confirmed by the hadith of the Prophet ﷺ:

> Islam shall be on the rise until traders take to the sea [carrying it], and horses charge in the cause of Allah. After that, a people will come and recite the Qur'an, saying: '*Who*

---

[1] Muhammad b. Ibrahim al-Shaybani and Ahmad al-Khazindar, eds. *Dalil Makhtutat al-Suyuti*, 2nd ed. (Kuwait: *Manshurat Markaz al-Makhtutat*, 1995).

*recites it better than us? Who is more knowledgeable than us?
Who is wiser than us?* Then he turned to his Companions
and asked: *'Is there any good in such as these?'* They said:
'Allah and His Prophet know best.' He said: *'Those are from
among you, O ummah! Those are fodder for the Fire.'*[2]

A reconciling factor is that the hadith of Ibn Abi Sulaym applies to
those who claim knowledge either undeservedly or proudly, and
not to those who act out of sincerity and obligation. Ibn 'Ata' Allah
said in his *hikam*:

> The root of every disobedience, forgetfulness, and desire
> is contentment with the self, while the root of every
> obedience, vigilance, and continence is your dissatisfaction
> with it. That you accompany an ignorant who is not
> pleased with himself is better for you than to accompany
> a knowledgeable person who is pleased with himself.
> And what ignorance is that of one who is dissatisfied with
> himself? And what knowledge is that of one who is satisfied
> with himself?

Imam al-Sha'rani in *al-'uhud al-muhammadiyya* ('The Pledges We
Made to the Prophet ﷺ') made a similar statement:

> The Prophet ﷺ took our pledge that we should not claim
> to possess knowledge except for a licit cause, and that we
> should never say: *'We are the most knowledgeable of people'*
> neither with our mouths nor with our hearts. How could
> we say such a thing when we know full well that in our
> country, let alone our region, there is one who is more
> knowledgeable than we? But if it is one day ordained for
> us to claim knowledge, then we must immediately follow
> this with repentance and ask forgiveness, lest punishment
> descend on us. This is a problem which no wise person
> ever faces, for there is no science which one has looked
> up, except the scholars of knowledge anticipated him and
> wrote books about it, scholars whose pupil he may not even
> deserve to be.

---

[2] Narrated from 'Umar by al-Bazzar with a sound chain as stated by Haythami.

Al-Suyuti's student and biographer Shams al-Din al-Dawudi al-Maliki, the author of *tabaqat al-mufassirin al-kubra*, said: '*I saw the sheikh with my own eyes writing and finishing three works in one day which he himself authored and proofread. At the same time, he was dictating hadith and replying beautifully to whatever was brought to his attention.*' Al-Sakhawi reproached him for his plagiarism of earlier books, and others added that the profusion of his works were the reason they were often incomplete, and for the frequency of flaws and contradictions in them. This is a charge commonly laid at the door of prolific authors, such as Ibn al-Jawzi and Ibn Taymiyyah. Also note that there was some animosity between al-Suyuti and his sheikh, al-Sakhawi, as exhibited in the former's tract *al-kawi fi al-radd 'ala al-sakhawi* ('The Searing Brand in Refuting al-Sakhawi') and his unflattering mention in the poem *nazm al-'iqyan fi a'yan al-a'yan.*

His chain of transmission in *tasawwuf* goes back to Sheikh 'Abd al-Qadir al-Jilani. Al-Suyuti belonged to the Shadhili *tariqa*, which he eulogized in his brief defence of *tasawwuf* entitled *tashyid al-haqiqa al-'aliyya*. In the book, he states: '*I have looked at the matters which the Imams of Shariah have criticized in Sufis, and I did not see a single true Sufi holding such positions. Rather, they are held by the people of innovation and the extremists who have claimed for themselves the title of Sufi while in reality they are not.*' In the *tashyid* he also produces narrative chains of transmission proving that al-Hasan al-Basri did in fact narrate directly from 'Ali ibn Abi Talib ﷺ. This goes against the commonly received opinion among the scholars of hadith[3] although it was also the opinion of Imam Ahmad ibn Hanbal.[4]

---

[3] See, for example, al-Sakhawi's words in his *Maqasid*, in the entry *khirqa*.

[4] Ibn Abi Ya'la, *tabaqat al-hanabila* (1:192): 'My father (Qadi Abu Ya'la) narrated to me in writing, "Isa ibn Muhammad ibn 'Ali narrated to us: I heard 'Abdullah ibn Muhammad (Imam Abu al-Qasim al-Baghawi) say: I heard Abu 'Abdullah Ahmad ibn Muhammad ibn Hanbal say: 'al-Hasan did narrate (*qad rawa*) from 'Ali ibn Abi Talib.'"' 'Abd al-Razzaq in his *Musannaf* (7:412) narrates that 'Ali even consulted al-Hasan in a certain judicial case. For the listing of the chains of transmission establishing that al-Hasan narrated from 'Ali see al-Suyuti's *ta'yid al-haqiqa al-'aliyya wa tashyid al-tariqa al-shadhiliyya* and Ahmad al-Ghumari's *al-burhan al-jali fi tahqiq intisab al-sufiyya ila 'ali*.

When one of his sheikhs, Burhan al-Din Ibrahim b. 'Umar al-Biqa'i (d. 885), attacked Ibn 'Arabi in a tract entitled *tanbih al-ghabi ila takfir Ibn 'Arabi* ('Warning to the Dolt That Ibn 'Arabi is an Apostat'), al-Suyuti countered with a tract entitled *tanbih al-ghabi fi takhti'a Ibn 'Arabi* ('Warning to the Dolt That Faults Ibn 'Arabi'). Both epistles have been published.[5] In his reply, al-Suyuti states that he considers Ibn 'Arabi a Friend of Allah whose writings are forbidden to those who read them without first learning the technical terms used by the Sufis. He cites from Ibn Hajar's list in *anba' al-ghumr*, the trusted scholars who kept a good opinion of Ibn 'Arabi or counted him a wali: Ibn 'Ata' Allah al-Iskandari (d. 709), al-Yafi'i (d. 678), Ibn 'Abd al-Salam after the latter's meeting with al-Shadhili, Shihab al-Din Abu al-'Abbas Ahmad ibn Yahya al-Malwi al-Tilimsani (d. 776), Siraj al-Din Abu Hafs 'Umar ibn Ishaq al-Hindi al-Hanafi (d. 773) the author of *sharh al-hidaya* and *sharh al-'ayni*, Najm al-Din al-Bahi al-Hanbali (d. 802), al-Jabarti (d. 806), the major lexicographer al-Fayruzabadi (d. 818), Shams al-Din al-Bisati al-Maliki (d. 842), al-Munawi (d. 871), and others. Of note regarding the above is the abundant use of Ibn 'Arabi's sayings by al-Munawi in his commentary of al-Suyuti's *jami' al-saghir* entitled *fayd al-qadir*, and by Fayruzabadi in his commentary on Bukhari's *al-Sahih*.

Al-Suyuti was Ash'ari in his doctrine as shown in many of his works. In *masalik al-hunafa fi walidayy al-mustafa* ('Methods Of Those With Pure Belief Concerning the Parents of The Prophet 🕋') he says:

> The parents of the Prophet 🕋 died before he attained Prophethood, and there is no punishment for them. The Qur'an says '*We never punish until We send a messenger [whom they reject]*' (al-Isra' 17:15). Our Ash'ari Imams, among those in *kalam*, *usul*, and *fiqh*, agree on the statement that one who dies while *da'wah* has not reached

---

[5] Al-Biqa'i, *masra' al-tasawwuf aw tanbih al-ghabi ila takfir Ibn 'Arabi*, ed. 'Abd al-Rahman al-Wakil (Bilbis: *Dar al-Taqwa*, 1989); al-Suyuti, *tanbih al-ghabi fi takhti'a Ibn 'Arabi*, ed. 'Abd al-Rahman Hasan Mahmud (Cairo: *Maktaba al-Adab*, 1990).

him, dies saved. This has been explained by Imam al-Shafi'i as follows: *'some of the fuqaha' explained that the reason for the above is, such a person follows fitra (primordial disposition), and has not stubbornly refused nor rejected any Messenger.'*[6]

Al-Suyuti was taken to task for his claim that he was capable of independent scholarly exertion or *ijtihad mutlaq*. He explained:

I did not mean that I was similar to one of the Four Imams, but that I was an affiliated *mujtahid* (*mujtahid muntasib*). For, when I reached the level of *tarjih* or *distinguishing the best fatwa inside the school*, I did not contravene al-Nawawi's *tarjih*. And, when I reached the level of *ijtihad mutlaq*, I did not contravene al-Shafi'i's school.

He continued:

There is no one in our time, on the face of the earth, from East to West, more knowledgeable than me in Hadith and the Arabic language, save al-Khidr or the Pole of saints or some other wali—none of whom do I include into my statement—and Allah knows best.[7]

He also said *'When I went on hajj, I drank Zamzam water for several matters. Among them was that I reach the level of Sheikh Siraj al-Din al-Bulqini in fiqh, and in hadith, that of hafiz Ibn Hajar.'*[8]

---

[6] It is related that some of the Ash'ari imams such as al-Qurtubi, al-Subki, and al-Sha'rani said that Abu Talib, the Prophet's uncle, was also saved, according to Sheikh Ahmad Zayni Dahlan in his epistle *asna al-matalib fi najat Abi Talib* (Cairo: *Muhammad Effendi Mustafa*, 1305/1886) who cites Imam al-Suhaymi and the Hanafi Mufti of Mecca Sheikh Ahmad b. 'Abdullah Mirghani to that effect. They mention, among other evidence, the narration of al-'Abbas ﷺ. Ibn Sa'd said in his *tabaqat al-kubra* (1:118): 'Affan b. Muslim told us: Hammad b. Salama told us: from Thabit [ibn Aslam al-Bunani]: from Ishaq b. 'Abdullah b. al-Harith [ibn Nawfal] who said: al-'Abbas said: 'I said: "O Messenger of Allah, do you hope anything for Abu Talib?" He replied: "I hope everything good from my Lord."' The above narrators are all trustworthy and their transmission is sound, except that the meaning of the hadith is vague. Further, al-Qurtubi, in his *tafsir* (for verses 6:26 and 9:53) and Ibn al-Subki in *tabaqat al-shafi'iyya al-kubra* (1:91-94) hold different positions than those ascribed to them above, and the sound evidence to the contrary is explicit and abundant, but Allah knows best.

[7] Al-Suyuti, *al-radd 'ala man akhlada ila al-ard* (p. 116).

[8] Al-Suyuti, *husn al-muhadara fi akhbar misr wa al-qahira* (p. 157).

Below are the titles of some of al-Suyuti's works in print, kept in the Arabic collection of the University of Princeton in the State of New Jersey (USA). The most recent date has been given for works with more than one edition:

1. *abwab al sa'ada fi asbab al-shahada* <1987>
   ('The Gates of Felicity in the Causes of the Witnessing to Oneness')
2. *al-ashbah wa al-naza'ir fi furu' al-shafi'iyya*
   ('Similarities in the Branches of the Law Within the Shafi'i School')
3. *al-ashbah wa al-naza'ir fi al-'arabiyya*
   ('Similarities in Arabic')
4. *al-ahadith al-hisan fi fadl al-taylasan* <1983>
   ('The Beautiful Narrations on the Merit of the Male Head-covering')
5. *al-fawz al-'azim fi liqa' al-karim* <1994>
   ('The Tremendous Victory in Meeting the All-Generous')
6. *alfiyya al-suyuti al-nahwiyya* <1900>
   ('The Thousand-Line Poem on Philology')
7. *alfiyya al-suyuti fi mustalah al-hadith* <1988>
   ('The Thousand-Line Poem on Hadith Nomenclature')
8. *'amal al-yawm wa al-layla* <1987>
   ('Supererogatory Devotions for Each Day and Night')
9. *al-itqan fi 'ulum al-qur'an* <1996>
   ('Precision and Mastery in the Sciences of the Qur'an')
10. *anis al-jalis* <1874> ('The Familiar Companion')
11. *al-'araj fi al-faraj* <1988> ('A Commentary on Ibn Abi al-Dunya's "The Deliverance"', a work on hope and joy)
12. *al-arba'un hadith fi qawa'id al-ahkam al-shar'iyya* <1986>
    ('Forty Narrations on Basic Legal Rulings')
13. *asbab al-nuzul* <1983>
    ('Causes of Qur'anic Revelation', verse by verse)
14. *asbab wurud al-hadith* <1988>
    ('Causes and Circumstances of Hadith')
15. *isbal al-kisa' 'ala al-nisa'* <1984>
    ('Women and the Donning of Cover')
16. *asrar tartib al-Qur'an* <1976>
    ('The Secret in the Ordering of the Qur'an')
17. *al-ayat al-kubra fi sharh qissat al-isra'* <1985> ('The Great Sign: Commentary on the Story of the Night Journey of the Prophet ﷺ')

18. *'ayn al-isaba fi istidrak 'A'ishah 'ala al-Sahaba* <1988>
    ('Exactitude Itself in 'A'isha's Rectification of the Companions')
19. *azhar al-mutanathira fi al-ahadith al-mutawatira* <1951>
    ('The Most Prominent of the Reports Concerning the Narrations of
    Mass Transmission')
20. *al-bahir fi hukm al-nabi* 🕌 <1987>
    ('The Dazzling Light of the Rulings of the Prophet 🕌')
21. *al-bahja al-mardiyya fi sharh al-alfiyya* <1980> ('The pleasing beauty:
    a commentary on Muhammad Ibn 'Abdullah Ibn Malik's (d. 1274
    CE) "*Alfiyya*"', a thousand-line poem on grammar)
22. *bulbul al-rawda* <1981> ('Chronicle on al-Rawda, Egypt')
23. *bushra al-ka'ib bi liqa' al-Habib* <1960>
    ('The consolation of the sad with the meeting of the Beloved')
24. *al-dibaj 'ala sahih Muslim ibn al-Hajjaj* <1991>
    ('Two-volume commentary on Sahih Muslim')
25. *al-durar al-muntathira fi al-ahadith al-mushtahara* <1988> ('The
    scattered pearls of famous narrations'); also published as *al-nawafih
    al-'atira fi al-ahadith al-mushtahara* <1992> ('The fragrant scents of
    famous narrations')
26. *al-durr al-manthur fi al-tafsir bi al-ma'thur* ('The scattered pearls:
    A commentary of Qur'an based on transmitted reports')
27. *al-duruj al-munifa fi al-aba' al-sharifa* <1916> ('The outstanding
    entries concerning the ancestors of the Prophet 🕌 ')
28. *fadd al-wi'a' fi ahadith raf' al-yadayn fi al-du'a'* <1985> ('The
    emptying of the vessel concerning raising the hands when making
    supplication')
29. *al-ghurar fi fada'il 'Umar* <1991>
    ('The blazing highlights of Umar's merits')
30. *al-haba'ik fi akhbar al-mala'ik* <1985>
    ('The celestial orbits or the reports concerning the angels')
31. *haqiqa al-sunna wa al-bid'a aw al-'amr bi al-ittiba' wa al-nahi 'an al-
    munkar* <1985> ('The reality of Sunna and innovation or the ordering
    of obedient following and the prohibition of evil')
32. *al-hawi lil-fatawi fi al-fiqh wa-'ulum al-tafsir wa al-hadith wa al-usul
    wa-al-nahw wa al-i'rab wa-sa'ir al-funun* <1933> ('The collected legal
    decisions in jurisprudence, Qur'anic commentary, hadith, principles,
    language, and other sciences')

33. *al-hujaj al-mubayyana fi al-tafdil bayna makka wa al-madina* <1985> ('The proofs made manifest concerning the super excellence of Makkah and Madinah')

34. *husn al-maqsid fi 'amal al-mawlid* <1985> ('Excellence of purpose in celebrating the birth of the Prophet 📿')

35. *husn al-samt fi al-samt* <1985> ('The merits of silence')

36. *ihya' al-mayyit bi fadail ahl al-bayt* <1988> ('Giving life to the dead with the merits of the Family of the Prophet 📿')

37. *ikhtilaf al-madhahib* <1989> ('The divergences among the schools of law')

38. *al-iklil fi istinbat al-tanzil* <1981> ('The Diadem: the extraction of rulings from the revealed Book')

39. *inbah al-adhkiya' fi hayat al-anbiya'* <1916> ('Notice to the wise concerning the lives of the Prophets [i.e. In the grave]')

40. *sl-iqtirah fi 'ilm usul al-nahw* <1978> ('The authoritative discourse concerning the science of philology')

41. *al-izdihar fi ma 'aqadahu al-shu'ara min al-ahadith wa al-athar* <1991> ('The flourishes of poets related to the Prophetic narrations and sayings of the Companions')

42. *jam' al-jawami' al-ma'ruf bi al-jami' al-kabir* <1970> ('The collection of collections, known as the Major Collection')

43. *jami' al-ahadith al-jami' al-saghir wa zawa'idi* <1994> ('The Minor Collection and its addenda')

44. *jany al-jinas* <1986> ('The genera of rhetoric')

45. *jazil al-mawahib fi ikhtilaf al-madhahib* <1992> ('The abundant gifts concerning the differences among the schools of law')

46. *al-kanz al-madfun wa al-falak al-mashhun* <1992> ('The buried treasure in the laden ship: An encyclopedia of Islamic history')

47. *kashf al-salsala 'an wasf al-zalzala* <1987> ('The transmitted expositions concerning the description of the Earthquake of Doomsday')

48. *al-Radd 'ala man akhlada ila al-ardi wa jahila anna al-ijtihada fi kulli 'asrin fard* <1984> ('Refutation of those who cling to the earth and ignore that scholarly striving is a religious obligation in every age')

49. *kitab al-shamarikh fi 'ilm al-tarikh* <1894> ('The book of date-heavy stalks: a primer on historiography')

50. *kitab al-shihab al-thaqib fi dhamm al-khalil* <1992> ('The piercing arrows, a commentary on 'Ali ibn Zafir's (d. 1226 CE) "The Healing of

the Parched concerning the castigation of one's dear friend"', a book
on the ethics of friendship)

51. *kitab al-tabarri min ma'arra al-ma'arri wa tuhfa al- zurafa' bi asma'
    al-khulafa'* <1989> ('Poetry on the names of the Caliphs')
52. *kitab al-tadhkir bi al-marji' wa al-masir* <1991>
    ('Book of the reminder of the Return to Allah')
53. *kitab asma' al-mudallisin* <1992>
    ('The book of narrators who omit certain details while narrating')
54. *kitab bughya al-wu'a fi tabaqat al-lughawiyyin* <1908>
    ('The must of the sagacious concerning the biographical
    layers of lexicologists and philologists')
55. *kitab ham' al-hawami' sharh jam' al-jawami' fi 'ilm al-nahw* <1973>
    ('The rushing floodgates, or commentary on the Collection of
    collections on the science of philology')
56. *kitab husn al-muhadara fi akhbar misr wa al-qahira* <1904>
    ('The excellent lectures concerning the chronicle of Egypt and Cairo')
57. *kitab itmam al-diraya li qurra' al-nuqaya* <1891>
    ('The perfection of knowledge for the elite among readers')
58. *kitab lubb al-lubab fi tahrir al-ansab* <1840>
    ('The kernel of kernels concerning the editorship of genealogies')
59. *tazyin al-mamalik bi manaqib Imam Malik* <1907>
    ('The adornment of slaves with the virtues of Imam Malik')
60. *kitab tuhfat al-mujalis wa nuzha al-majalis* <1908>
    ('The jewel of every fellow student and the pleasant gatherings')
61. *laqat al-marjan fi ahkam al-jan* <1989>
    ('The gleanings of coral: rulings concerning the jinn')
62. *lubab al-nuqul fi asbab al-nuzul* <1981>
    ('The best of narrations concerning the circumstances of revelation')
63. *al-luma' fi khasa'is yawm al-jumu'ah* <1986>
    ('The merits of The day of jumu'ah')
64. *ma rawahu al-asatin fi 'adam al-maji' ila al-salatin* <1992> ('The
    reports concerning not appearing at the courts of rulers'); together
    with *dhamm al-maks* ('The blame of taxes and tolls')
65. *manahil al-safa fi takhrij ahadith al-shifa* <1988>
    ('The Springs of Purity: Documentation of the hadiths mentioned in
    Qadi 'Iyad's "The Healing"')
66. *manaqib al-khulafa' al-rashidin* <1890>
    ('Virtues of the well-guided Caliphs')

67. *al-manhaj al-sawi wa al-manhal al-rawi fi al-tibb al-nabawi* <1986>
('The straight path & quenching spring: the Prophetic medicine ﷺ)
68. *al-maqamat al-sundusiyya fi al-nisba al-mustafawiyya* <1916>
('The resplendent stations concerning Prophetic ancestry')
69. *al-masabih fi salat al-tarawih* <1955>
('The lanterns of the "prayer of rests" [tarawih]')
70. *masalik al-hunafa' fi waliday al-Mustafa* <1993> ('Method of those
of pure religion concerning the parents of the Prophet ﷺ')
71. *al-matali' al-sa'ida fi sharh al-Suyuti 'ala al-alfiyya al-musamma bi
al-farida fi al-nahw wa al-tasrif wa al-khatt* <1981>
('Suyuti's commentary on his own thousand-line poem entitled "The
unique pearl" on philology, conjugation, and calligraphy')
72. *matla' al-badrayn fiman yu'ta ajrahu marratayn* <1991>
('The rising of the two full moons: those who are rewarded
twice [i.e. Sincere Christians who accept Islam]')
73. *miftah al-jannah fi al-i'tisam bi al-sunnah* <1993> ('The key to
paradise which consists in clinging to the Sunnah of the Prophet ﷺ')
74. *mufhimat al-aqran fi mubhamat al-Qur'an* <1991>
('The elucidations of the peers for the obscurities of the Qur'an')
75. *al-muhadhdhab fima waqa' fi al-Qur'an min al-mu'arrab* <1988>
('The emendation concerning foreign words & phrases in the Qur'an')
76. *mu'jiza ma'a karama fi kitab al-sharaf al-muhattam: fi ma manna
Allah ta'ala bihi 'ala waliyyihi Ahmad al-Rifa'i* <1965> ('The miracle
and gift concerning the book of "The paramount honour" [by al-
Rifa'i] and what Allah has bestowed in it upon His Friend Ahmad
[ibn 'Ali] al-Rifa'i [d. 1182 CE]')
77. *mukhtasar sharh al-jami' al-saghir li al-munawi* <1954>
('The abridged commentary of the minor collection by al-Munawi')
78. *muntaha al-'amal fi sharh hadith innama al-a'mal* <1986>
('The goal of all practice, or the commentary on the hadith: Actions
are according to intentions')
79. *musnad Fatima al-zahra' radiya allah anha wa ma warada fi
fadliha*<1994> ('The narrations traced back to Fatima the Radiant
and the reports concerning her virtues')
80. *mustazraf min akhbar al-jawari* <1989>
('The graceful reports concerning women slaves')
81. *mutawakkili fima warada fi al-Qur'an bi al-lugha al-Habashiyya
wa al-Farisiyya wa al-Rumiyya wa al-Hindiyya wa al-Siryaniyya wa*

al-'Ibraniyya wa al-Nabatiyya wa al-Qibtiyya wa al-Turkiyya wa al-Zanjiyya wa al-Barbariyya ('My reliance concerning what has been mentioned in the Qur'an in Ethiopian, Farsi, Greek, Hindi, Syriac, Hebrew, Nabatean, Coptic, Turkic, African, and Berber')

82. *nashr al-'alamayn al-munifayn fi ihya' al-abawayn al-sharifayn* <1916> ('The proclamation to the two outstanding worlds [mankind & jinn] concerning the resuscitation of the parents of the Prophet ﷺ')

83. *natija al-fikr fi al-jahr bi al-dhikr* <1950> ('The conclusion of reflection upon loud remembrance of Allah')

84. *nazm al-'iqyan fi a'yan al-a'yan* <1927> ('Who's who in the ninth Hijri century')

85. *al-Nukat al-badi'at 'ala al-mawdu'at* <1991> (al-Suyuti's critique of Ibn al-Jawzi's collection of forged narrations)

86. *nuzha al-julasa' fi ash'ar al-nisa'* <1986> ('The recreation of student gatherings concerning famous women poets')

87. *nuzha al-muta'ammil wa-murshid al-muta'ahhil: fi al-khatib wa-al-mutazawwij* <1989> ('The recreation of the fiancé and the guide of the married')

88. *nuzha al-'umr fi al-tafdil bayna al-bayd wa al-sumr* <1931> ('The recreation of life about establishing preference between the white and the black in complexion')

89. *nuzul 'Isa ibn Maryam Akhir al-Zaman* <1985> ('The descent of 'Isa ibn Maryam at the end of time')

90. *al-qawl al-jali fi fada'il 'Ali* <1990> ('The manifest discourse on the virtues of 'Ali ibn Abi Talib radiyallahu 'anhu')

91. *al-rahma fi al-tibb wa al-hikma* <1970> ('Arabic medicine and wisdom')

92. *al-rasa'il al-'ashr* <1989> ('The ten epistles')

93. *rasf al-la'al fi wasf al-hilal* <1890> ('The stringing of the pearls in describing the new moon')

94. *al-rawd al-aniq fi fadl al-siddiq* <1990> ('The beautiful garden of the merit of Abu Bakr al-Siddiq radiyallahu 'anhu')

95. *risala al-sayf al-qati' al-lami' li ahl al-i'tirad al-shawa'i'* <1935> ('Epistle of the sharp and glistening sword to the Shi'i people of opposition')

96. *al-riyad al-aniqa fi sharh asma' khayr al-khaliqa sallallahu 'alayhi wa sallam* ('The beautiful gardens: explanation of the names of the Best of Creation [the Prophet Muhammad ﷺ]')

97. *sawn al-mantiq wa al-kalam 'an fann al-mantiq wa al-kalam* <1947> ('Manual of logic and dialectic theology')
98. *shaqa'iq al-utruj fi raqa'iq al-ghunj* <1988> ('The citron halves: or, the delicacy of women')
99. *sharh al-sudur bi sharh hal al-mawta wa al-qubur* <1989> ('Expanding of breasts or exegesis on the state of the dead in the grave')
100. *sharh al-urjuza al-musamma bi 'uqud al-juman fi 'alam al-ma'ani wa al-bayan* <1955> ('The commentary in rajaz [surging] meter entitled: The pearl necklaces related to the world of meanings and precious discourse')
101. *sharh shawahid al-mughni* <1904> ('Commentary on the proof-texts of 'Abdullah ibn Hisham's (d. 1360CE) *mughni al-labib* or "The sufficient knowledge of the sensible one"')
102. *shurut al-mufassir wa adabuh* <1994> ('The criteria to be met by commentators of Qur'an and their ethics')
103. *siham al-isaba fi al-da'awat al-mujaba* <1987> ('The arrows that hit their target: About the prayers that are fulfilled')
104. *subul al-jaliyya fi al-aba' al-'aliyya* <1916> ('The manifest paths concerning the lofty ancestors [of the Prophet 壡]')
105. *ta'aqqubat al-Suyuti 'ala mawdu'at Ibn al-Jawzi* <1886> ('Suyuti's critique of Ibn al-Jawzi's collection of forged narrations')
106. *tabaqat al-mufassirin* <1976> ('The biographical layers of Qur'an commentators')
107. *tabyid al-sahifa bi manaqib al-imam Abi Hanifa* <1992> ('The whitening of the page: or, the virtues of Imam Abu Hanifa')
108. *al-tadhyil wa al-tadhnib 'ala al-Nihaya fi gharib al-hadith wa al-athar* <1982> ('Marginal annotations on Ibn al-Athir's "The goal"')
109. *tadrib al-rawi fi sharh taqrib al-nawawi* <1994> ('The training of the hadith transmitter: an exegesis of Nawawi's "The facilitation"')
110. *tahdhib al-khasa'is al-nabawiyya al-kubra* <1989> ('The emendation of al-Suyuti's book entitled "The Awesome Characteristics of the Prophet 壡"')
111. *tahdhir al-khawas min akadhib al-qussas* <1932> ('Warning the elite against the lies of story-tellers')
112. *takhrij ahadiith sharh al-mawaqif fi 'ilm al-kalam* <1986> ('The documentation of the hadiths mentioned in "The commentary of the stopping-places in dialectical theology", a work by Qadi 'Adud al-Din 'Abd al-Rahman ibn Ahmad Ayji al-Shirazi (d. 756)

113. *tamhid al-farsh fi al-khisal al-mujiba li-zilal al-'arsh* <1990> ('The characteristics that guarantee the shading of the Throne')

114. *tanbih al-ghabi fi takhti'a ibn 'Arabi* <1990> ('Warning to the ignorant who imputes error to Muhyi al-Din Ibn 'Arabi' [a reply to al-Biqa'i's 'Warning of the ignorant that Ibn 'Arabi is a disbeliever]')

115. *tanwir al-hawalik sharh 'ala muwatta' Malik* <1969> ('The enlightenment of intense blackness: a commentary on Malik's "Trodden path"'); together with Is'af al-mubatta' fi rijal al-muwatta' ('The succor of the stalled concerning the narrators of Malik's "Trodden Path"')

116. *tanwir al-miqbas min tafsir ibn 'Abbas* <1951> ('The enlightenment of torchlights from the Qur'anic commentary of Ibn 'Abbas')

117. *tanzih al-anbiya' 'an tashbih al-aghbiya'* <1916> ('Declaring the Prophets far above the comparisons ignorant people make of themselves with them')

118. *taqrir al-istinad fi tafsir al-ijtihad* <1983> ('Establishing authoritative ascription in the course of scholarly striving')

119. *al-ta'rif bi adab al-ta'lif* <1989> ('The etiquette of authorship')

120. *tarikh al-khulafa'* <1993> ('History of the Caliphs')

121. *tartib suwar al-qur'an* <1986>
('The disposition of the surahs of the Qur'an')

122. *tasliya al-aba' bi-fuqdan al-abna' al-musamma al-ta'allul wa al-itfa' li-nar la tutfa'* <1987> ('The consolation of parents who have lost their children' also known as 'The extinction of the fire that cannot be extinguished')

123. *tawq al-hamama* <1988> ('The flight of the dove')

124. *ta'yid al-haqiqa al-'aliyya wa tashyid al-tariqa al-shadhiliyya* <1934> ('The upholding of the lofty truth and the buttressing of the Shadhili sufi path')

125. *al-ta'zim wa al-minna fi anna abaway rasulallah fi al-jannah* <1916> ('That the parents of the Prophet ﷺ are in Paradise')

126. *tuhfa al-abrar bi nukat al-adhkar li al-nawawi* <1990>
('Commentary on Nawawi's "Supplications"')

127. *tuhfa al-'ajlan fi fada'il 'Uthman* <1991>
('The merits of 'Uthman ibn 'Affan')

128. *tuhfa al-nujaba'* <1990>
('The gem of patricians [a work on language]')

129. *'uqud al-zabarjad 'ala musnad al-Imam Ahmad* <1987> ('The chrysolite necklaces on Imam Ahmad's collection of narrations traced to the Prophet ﷺ')
130. *'uqud al-zabarjad fi i'r'ab al-hadith al-nabawi* <1994> ('The chrysolite necklaces on the grammatical analysis of the narrations of the Prophet ﷺ')
131. *al-wasa'il fi musamara al-awa'il* <1986> ('The means for conversation with the ancients'); also published as al-Wasa'il ila Ma'rifa al-Awa'il <1990> ('The means to the acquaintance of the ancients')
132. *wusul al-amani bi usul al-tahani* <1987> ('The attainment of one's hope in the etiquette of well-wishing')
133. *al-zajr bi al-hijr* <1950> ('The reprimand by means of the reminder of what is unlawful')
134. *zubda al-laban fawa'id lughawiyya wa hadithiyya* <1989> ('Cream of the Milk: miscellaneous benefits related to language & hadith')
135. *akhlaq hamalat al-qur'an* <1987> ('Manners of the carriers of Qur'an')
136. *badhl al-himma fi talab bara'a al-dhimma* ('Directing one's energies to pursue clearness of conscience'); contained in the collective volume entitled: *thalath rasa'il fi al-ghiba* <1988> ('Three epistles on slander')
137. *al-la'ali' al-masnu'a fi al-ahadith al-mawdu'a* <1960> ('The artificial pearls or forged hadiths')
138. *daqa'iq al-akhbar fi dhikr al-jannah wa al-nar* <1961> ('The subtleties in the reports that mention Paradise and the Fire')
139. *al-ithaf bi hubb al-ashraf* <1900> ('The present concerning love of the nobility [i.e. Descendants of the Prophet ﷺ]')
140. *hay'a al-saniyya fi al-hay'a al-sunniyya* <1982> ('Treatise on astronomy')

Main sources: Ibn Fahd, *Dhayl Tadhkira al-Huffaz* p. 6-10; al-Suyuti, *Tarikh al-Khulafa'*, introduction p. 5-10; Nuh Keller, *Reliance of the Traveller* p. 1100.

يَٰٓأَيُّهَا ٱلَّذِينَ ءَامَنُوا۟

ٱتَّقُوا۟ ٱللَّهَ حَقَّ تُقَاتِهِۦ

O you who believe,
be mindful of Allah, as is His due,
ĀL ʿIMRAN:102

مَا رَوَاهُ الأَسَاطِينُ فِي عَدَمِ الْمَجِيءِ إِلَى السَّلَاطِينَ

ALL THE SULTAN'S MEN

Being a Translation of Imam Jalal al-Din al-Suyuti's
ma rawahu al-asatin fi 'adam al-maji' ila al-salatin

By the Polymath Mujtahid
JALAL AL-DIN AL-SUYUTI

Translation
TALUT DAWOOD

Imam Ghazali
INSTITUTE

In the Name of Allah, the Beneficent, the Merciful
All praise is due to Allah. And He is sufficient.
Peace be upon His chosen slaves. This is
'What the Distinguished Experts
Have Narrated Regarding
Never Visiting the
Rulers':

I

THE PROHIBITION OF VISITING
THE RULERS IN THE PROPHETIC SUNNAH

ABU DAWUD, AL-TIRMIDHI, AL-NASA'I, and al-Bayhaqi in *Shu'b al-Iman*, all narrated from Ibn 'Abbas ♦ that the Prophet ♦ said: '*Whoever lives in barren, desert lands becomes harsh, whoever follows hunting game becomes negligent, and whoever comes to the doors of the rulers is tried.*'

Abu Dawud and al-Bayhaqi narrated from Abu Hurayrah ♦ that the Prophet ♦ said, '*Whoever lives in the desert becomes harsh, whoever follows (hunting) game becomes negligent, and whoever comes to the doors of the rulers is tried. No slave is increased in nearness to the ruler, except that he is increased in remoteness from Allah.*'

Ahmad in his *Musnad*, and al-Bayhaqi with an authentic chain of transmission, narrated from Abu Hurayrah (radiyallahu 'anhu) that the Messenger of Allah ♦ said, '*Whoever lives in the desert becomes harsh, whoever follows [hunting] games becomes negligent, and whoever comes to the doors of the rulers is tried.*'

⚘

2

THE MOST HATED OF PEOPLE TO ALLAH ﷻ

IBN 'ADI HAS NARRATED FROM ABU HURAYRAH ﷺ that the Messenger of Allah ﷺ said, '*In Hell, there is a valley from which the Fire seeks refuge seventy times a day. Allah ﷻ has prepared it for the jurists who act to be admired by people. And the most hated of people to Allah ﷻ is the scholar of the ruler.*'

Ibn Bilal, Hafiz Abu al-Fityan al-Dahatnani, in the book *al-Tahdhir min 'Ulama' al-Su'*, and al-Rafi'i in *Tarikh Qazwin*, all narrated from Abu Hurayrah ﷺ that the Messenger of Allah ﷺ said, '*The most hated of people in the universe to Allah ﷻ is the scholar that visits the rulers.*'

The wording of Abu al-Fityan is: '*The most worthless of people to Allah, is the scholar that visits the rulers.*'

Ibn Majah narrated from Abu Hurayrah ﷺ that the Messenger of Allah ﷺ said, '*The most hated of reciters to Allah are those that visit the rulers.*'

Al-Daylami narrated in *Musnad al-Firdaws* from Abu Hurayrah ﷺ that the Messenger of Allah ﷺ said, '*If you see a scholar mixing frequently with the ruler, then know that he is a worldly person.*'

Ibn Majah narrated, with a chain of transmission to his trustworthy narrators, from Ibn 'Abbas ﷺ that the Prophet ﷺ said:

> There are people from my *ummah* that study the religion and recite the Qur'an. They will say, '*We go to the rulers for our share of this world. But we avoid them in our religious matters.*' However, that is not the case. Just as one who enters a thorny bush can expect to be pricked by a thorn, one can only expect to be afflicted with sinfulness from nearness to them.

Al-Tabarani narrated in his *Awsat*, with an authentic chain of transmission to his trustworthy narrators, from Thawban ﷺ, the freed slave of the Messenger of Allah ﷺ, that he said:

> 'O, Messenger of Allah! Am I from the people of your house?' But he remained silent. I asked him a second and third time. On the third, he said, 'Yes. As long as you do not remain near a fortified gate or go to the ruler seeking anything from him.'

Hafiz al-Mundhiri said, in *Al-Targhib wa al-Tarhib*, *'The meaning of "the fortified gate" is the gate of the ruler, or other leaders.'*

3

WILL THE PERSON WHO ENTERS UPON THE RULER DRINK FROM THE LAKE OF THE PROPHET ﷺ?

AL-NASA'I AND AL-BAYHAQI NARRATED, as well as al-Tirmidhi and al-Nasa'i, both of whom declared it authentic, from Ka'b ibn 'Ujrah ﷺ that the Messenger of Allah ﷺ said:

> There will be [corrupt] rulers after me. Whoever enters upon them, confirms their lies, and assists them in their oppression, has nothing to do with me and I have nothing to do with him. He will not come to my lake. But whoever does not enter upon them, does not assist them in their oppression, and does not confirm their lies, he is from me and I am from him. And he will come to my lake.

Ahmad, Abu Na'im, and Ibn Hibban, the latter in his *al-Sahih*, narrated from Abu Sa'id al-Khudri ﷺ that the Prophet ﷺ said:

> There will be governors that will be distracted by well-off and important people. They will lie and oppress. I am free from anyone who enters upon them, confirms their lies, and supports them in their oppression. And he is free from me. But if someone does not enter upon them, does not confirm their lies, and does not assist them in their oppression, he is from me and I am from him.

Ahmad and Ibn Hibban, the latter in his *al-Sahih*, narrated from Jabir ibn 'Abdullah ﷺ that the Messenger of Allah ﷺ said:

> There will be rulers who, if someone enters upon them, helps them in their profession, and confirms their lies, he is not

from me, nor am I from him. And he will not come to my lake. Those who do not enter upon them, do not assist them in their oppression, and do not confirm their lies, are from me, and I am from them. And they will come to my lake.

Al-Shirazi narrated in *Al-Alqab* that the Messenger of Allah said:

Indeed, there will be governors after me such that, whoever confirms their lies and supports them in their oppression, is not from me, and I am not from him. Nor will he come to my lake. Those who do not enter upon them, nor confirm their lies, nor support them in their oppression, nor approach their doors, are from me, and I am from them. They will come to my lake.

❈

4

THE JURISTS ARE THE CUSTODIANS OF THE MESSENGERS

AL-HASAN IBN SUFYAN IN HIS MUSNAD, al-Hakim in his *Tarikh*, Abu Na'im, al-Daylami, and al-Rafi'i in his *Tarikh*, narrated from Anas ibn Malik ﷺ that the Messenger of Allah ﷺ said, '*The scholars are the custodians of the Messengers as long as they do not mix with the ruler. In that case, they will have betrayed the trust of the Messengers. So, beware of them and keep away from them.*'

Al-'Askari narrated from 'Ali ibn Abi Talib ﷺ that the Messenger of Allah ﷺ said, '*The jurists are the custodians of the Messengers as long as they do not get involved in the world and follow the orders of the ruler. If they do that, then avoid them.*'

❀

5

THE SCHOLAR WILL HAVE THE SAME PUNISHMENT AS THE RULER

AL-HAKIM, IN HIS TARIKH, along with al-Daylami, narrated from Mu'adh ibn Jabal ☙ that the Messenger of Allah ﷺ said, '*No scholar comes to the ruler in obedience, except that he will be his partner in every category of punishment in the Hellfire.*'

Abu al-Shaykh narrated in *al-Thawab* from Mu'adh ibn Jabal ☙, that the Messenger of Allah ﷺ said, '*If a man recites the Qur'an and studies the jurisprudence of the religion, then comes to the ruler, adhering to him and desiring what is in his hands, he will plunge through the number of his mistakes into the Fire of Hell.*'

6

FROM THE ATTRIBUTES OF
THE SCHOLARS OF THE END TIMES

AL-DAYLAMI NARRATED FROM Ibn 'Abbas ☙ that the Messenger of
Allah ☙ said:

> In the End Times, there will be scholars who cause people
> to aspire for the Hereafter, yet they themselves will not
> aspire for it. They will command people to abstain from
> the world, yet they themselves will not abstain from it. And
> they will forbid people from frequenting the rulers but will
> not stop themselves.

Al-Daylami narrated from 'Umar ibn al-Khattab ☙ that the
Messenger of Allah ☙ said, '*Allah loves the rulers who mix with the
scholars and He hates the scholars who mix with the rulers. This is
because, when the scholars mix with the rulers, they become greedy
for the world, but when the rulers mix with the scholars, they aspire
for the Hereafter.*'

Abu 'Umar al-Mada'ini narrated in his *Kitab al-Fitan* from
al-Hasan that the Messenger of Allah ☙ said, '*This ummah will not
cease to be under Allah's safeguarding and protection as long as its
reciters do not incline towards its rulers.*'

Al-Hakim narrated, declaring it *sahih*, from 'Abdullah ibn
al-Shakhir that the Messenger of Allah ☙ said, '*Minimize your
visiting the rich. It is more effective in preventing you from minimizing
His favours.*'

Al-Hakim al-Tirmidhi narrated, in his *Nawadir al-Usul*, that
'Umar ibn al-Khattab ☙ said:

I came to the Messenger of Allah 🕋 and I noticed signs of anger on his face. He grabbed my beard and said, '*To Allah we belong and to Him we will return. Jibril came to me and said, "Your ummah will be tried shortly after you, not long after." I said, "Why is that?" He said, "Because of their reciters and their rulers, who will deny people their rights. They will never give them to them. The reciters will follow those rulers in that." I said, "O, Jibril! How can someone be safe from that?" He said, "By abstaining and being patient. If he is given his rights, he takes it. If he is denied his rights, he abandons it."'*

7

SEDITIOUS RULERS

AL-HAKIM NARRATED FROM 'Abdullah ibn al-Harith ﷺ that he heard the Messenger of Allah ﷺ saying, '*After me, there will be rulers who, strife will frequent their doors as a baby camel frequents his sleeping place. No one will be given anything [by them], except that he will be decreased in religion proportionately.*'

Al-Daylami narrated from Abu al-A'war al-Sulami that the Messenger of Allah ﷺ said:

> Beware of the doors of the rulers and their properties, for the closest of people to them is the furthest of them from Allah. If someone prefers the ruler to Allah, Allah will place strife in his heart, inwardly and outwardly. He will cause his scruples to depart and his bewilderment will leave him.

❁

8

PEOPLE WHO WILL STUDY THE JURISPRUDENCE OF THE RELIGION FOR THE GOODS OF THIS WORLD

IBN ʿASAKIR NARRATED FROM ʿIbn ʿAbbas 🙏 that the Messenger of Allah 🙏 said:

> After me, there will be a community among my ummah who will recite the Qur'an and study the jurisprudence of the religion. Then, Satan will come to them and say, '*If you were to go to the ruler, he would rectify your worldly affairs, and you may avoid him in the matters of your religion.*' However, that is not the case. If one enters a thorny bush, he can expect to get pricked. Likewise, one should only expect sinfulness to arise from being close to them.

9

THE RULING OF ONE WHO APPROACHES THE RULER THROUGH FLATTERY

HANAD IBN AL-SARI NARRATED IN AL-ZUHD from 'Ubayd Allah ibn 'Umayr that the Messenger of Allah ﷺ said, '*A man is not increased in nearness to the ruler, except that he is increased in remoteness from Allah.*'

Al-Daylami narrated from Anas ﷺ that the Messenger of Allah ﷺ said, '*If someone approaches the ruler an arm's length, he will be distanced from Allah a bow's length.*'

Al-Daylami narrated from Abu Darda' ﷺ that the Messenger of Allah ﷺ said:

> If someone walks to a tyrannical ruler, obeying him completely and flattering him when he enters his presence and greets him, he will plunge into the Hellfire for a time proportionate to the number of his sins until he returns from his presence to his home. If he inclines towards his desires, or is extreme in seeking his assistance, Allah will not place upon him (the ruler) any curse, except that upon that person will be a curse like it. And, he (the ruler) will not be punished in the Hellfire, with any kind of punishment, except that that person will have a similar punishment.

Abu al-Shaykh narrated from Ibn 'Umar ﷺ that the Messenger of Allah ﷺ said, '*If anyone recites the Qur'an and studies the rulings of the religion, then approaches the ruler desiring what is in his hands, his heart will be sealed. Every day, he will be punished with two kinds of punishment with which no one had been punished before.*'

Al-Hakim narrated in his *Tarikh* from Mu'adh ☬ that the Messenger of Allah ☬ said, '*If someone recites the Qur'an and studies the religious rulings, then approaches the ruler, he will plunge into the Hellfire proportionate to the sins of the ruler.*'

Al-Bayhaqi narrated, from a man from Bani Sulma, that the Messenger of Allah ☬ said, '*Beware of the doors of the ruler.*'

❀

10

WARNING AGAINST SITTING IN THE RULER'S GATHERING

AL-DAYLAMI NARRATED FROM ALI ☙ that the Messenger of Allah ☙ said, '*Beware of the gatherings of the ruler; it causes one's religion to leave him. And beware of his aid, that you may not praise his affair.*'

Ibn Abi Shaybah and al-Tabarani narrated from Ibn 'Abbas ☙ that the Messenger of Allah ☙ said, '*There will be rulers who you will recognize and those who you will deny. Whoever opposes them will be saved, whoever stays away from them will be safe, but whoever mixes with them will be destroyed.*'

Al-Bayhaqi narrated that Ibn Mas'ud ☙ said, '*At the door of the ruler, there is a temptation like that of the sleeping place of the baby camel. You will not receive any of their worldly goods, except that your religion will suffer proportionately.*'

Al-Darimi narrated in his *Musnad* that Ibn Mas'ud ☙ said, '*If someone wants to honour his religion, let him not visit the ruler, let him not be alone with [non-related] women, and let him not dispute with the people of desires.*'

※

II

THE ONE WHO VISITS THE RULER LOSES HIS RELIGION

AL-BUKHARI NARRATED IN HIS TARIKH, along with Ibn Sa'd in *al-Tabaqat*, that Ibn Mas'ud ﷺ said, '*A man will enter upon the ruler carrying his religion with him and he will exit having nothing with him.*'

Ibn Sa'd narrated in *al-Tabaqat* that Salamah ibn Nabit said:

I entered upon my father who had seen and witnessed the Prophet ﷺ and had learned from him. [I said] '*O, my father! If you would go to such-and-such a governor, you and your family will receive something from him.*' He said, '*O, my son! I fear that I may sit among them in a gathering that will enter me into the Fire.*'

12

BLAMEWORTHY TRAITS IN THE SEEKERS OF KNOWLEDGE

AL-DARIMI NARRATED THAT IBN MAS'UD ﷺ said, '*There are four things which, if anyone seeks knowledge for the sake of any of them, he will enter the Fire: to impress the scholars, to dispute with the ignorant, to turn people towards him, or to enter with it upon the rulers.*'

Ibn Majah and al-Bayhaqi narrated that Ibn Mas'ud ﷺ said:

> If the people of knowledge would protect knowledge and only give it to those deserving of it, they would gain influence of the people of their age. However, they spread it to the people of the world in order to obtain the goods of this world. Thus, they (the people) despise them. I heard your Prophet ﷺ say, '*If someone limits himself to a solitary worry—the preoccupation with his Hereafter—Allah will suffice him for the affairs of his worldly life that preoccupy him. However, if someone is consumed with preoccupation for the affairs of this world, Allah will not care in what valley he destroys him.*'

Ibn Abi Shaybah narrated that Hudhayfah ibn al-Yaman ﷺ said, '*Nay! Let no man among you take a single step towards the ruler.*'

❈

13

BEWARE OF GOING
HEADLONG INTO SEDITION

IBN ABI SHAYBAH, AL-BAYHAQI, AND ABU NA'IM all narrated,
the latter in *al-Hilyah*, that Hudhayfah ﷺ said, '*Beware of the
endorsement of sedition.*' It was said, '*What is the endorsement of
sedition?*' He said, '*The doors of the ruler and the governors. One of
you may enter upon the governor, confirm his lies, and speak what
he does not believe.*'

Ibn Hisham narrated from Abu Umamah al-Bahili ﷺ that the
Messenger of Allah ﷺ said, '*The most hated of people to Allah,
is a man who sits in the gathering of the governors and confirms
whatever false words they speak.*'

14

THE COUNSEL
OF WAHB IBN MUNABBIH TO 'ATA'

AL-BAYHAQI NARRATED THAT WAHB IBN MUNABBIH said, *'O, 'Ata'!*
Beware of the doors of the rulers. For the doors of the rulers are
a sedition, like the sleeping place of a camel. You will not obtain
anything of their worldly goods, except that your religion will suffer
proportionately.'

Ibn Abi Shaybah narrated that Salamah ibn Qays said:

> I met Abu Dharr and he said, *'O, Salamah ibn Qays!*
> *Memorize three things: Do not marry more than one wife*
> *at a time, for you will never be able to be fair even if you are*
> *eager to do so. Do not work in charity, for the charity worker*
> *may make mistakes. And do not frequent the door of the*
> *ruler, for you will not receive anything from their worldly*
> *life, except that your religion will suffer proportionately.'*

Al-Bayhaqi narrated from Ayyub al-Sakhtiyani that Abu Qalabah
said, *'Memorize three things from me: Beware of the doors of the*
ruler; beware of sitting with the people of desires; and tend to your
own affairs, because independence is part of wellbeing.'

❀

15
Do Not Sit
with Heretical People

AL-BAYHAQI NARRATED, by way of Hammad ibn Salamah, that Yunus ibn 'Ubayd said, '*Do not sit with heretical people, do not keep the company of the ruler, and never be alone with a [non-related] woman.*'

Al-Bayhaqi narrated that al-Fadl ibn 'Abbas ﷺ said, '*We used to learn to keep away from rulers the way that we learned the surahs of the Qur'an.*' Al-Bayhaqi narrated that Yusuf ibn Asbat said:

> Sufyan al-Thawri said to me, '*If you see a reciter seeking refuge with the ruler, then know that he is a thief. If you see him seeking refuge with the rich, know that he is a show-off. And, beware of being enticed by someone saying to you, "You will be able to transmit people's complaints or defend an oppressed person." That is the beguilement that Iblis uses as a steppingstone [to deceive the reciters].*'

Al-Bayhaqi narrated that Abu Shihab said, '*I heard Sufyan al-Thawri say to a man, "If they call upon you to recite to them even one verse, do not go to them." It was said to Abu Shihab, "Who do you mean?" He replied, "The ruler."*'

And he (al-Bayhaqi) narrated that Anas ﷺ said, '*I met ten or so men from the tabi'in who all said, "Do not go to them and do not command them", meaning the ruler.*'

⚜

16

BEWARE OF DESIRES AND DISPUTES

AL-BAYHAQI NARRATED that Ahmad ibn 'Ubayd Allah said, '*I heard a man asking al-Shuri to counsel him. He said, "Beware of desires, and beware of the rulers."*'

Al-Bayhaqi narrated that Bakr ibn Muhammad al-'Abid said, '*I heard Sufyan al-Thawri say, "In Hell, there is a valley from which Hell seeks refuge seventy times a day. Allah has prepared it for the jurists who visit the rulers."*'

Abu Na'im narrated in *al-Hilyah*, by way of Hisham ibn 'Abbad, who said, '*I heard Ja'far ibn Muhammad say, "The jurists are the custodians of the Messengers. So, if you see that the jurists have inclined towards the rulers, then treat them with suspicion."*'

Ibn Najjar narrated in his *Tarikh*, by way of Ibn Darid, that it was said to Jabir ibn Hayyan, '*Why do you never go to the rulers?*' He said, '*I am sufficed by the One for whose sake I have left them.*'

Al-Khatib al-Baghdadi narrated in his *Tarikh* by way of Ibn Darid, from Abu Hatim, from al-Qa'nabi that his father said:

> 'Isa ibn Musa said to Ibn Shibrimah, at the time that the former was governor of Kufah, '*Why do you not come to visit us?*' He said, '*May Allah rectify you. If I were to visit you, and you were to draw me close, I would be tried. And if you were to distance me, you would harm me. Furthermore, I do not have anything that I fear losing, nor do you have anything that I hope for.*' He did not reply to this.

Al-Rafi'i narrated in Tarikh Qazwin that 'Abdullah ibn al-Sada said, '*Abu Bakr ibn 'Iyash wrote to 'Abdullah ibn al-Mubarak, "If al-Fadl ibn Musa al-Shaybani does not visit the rulers, then transmit my greeting to him."*'

NOTE: The majority of the scholars of the Predecessors and the pious among the later generations were of the opinion that these hadiths and narrations should be taken in their general sense, without regard for whether or not they (the rulers) have summoned one to themselves, and without regard for whether they have called one for a sound religious purpose or not.

Sufyan al-Thawri said, '*If they should call you to recite even a single verse to them, do not go to them.*' This is narrated by al-Bayhaqi, as previously mentioned.

17

THE STATES OF THE PIOUS PREDECESSORS REGARDING THE GOVERNORS

ABU NA'IM NARRATED IN AL-HILYAH, from Maymun ibn Mahran, that 'Abd al-Malik ibn Marwan arrived in Madinah and sent one of his gatekeepers to Sa'id ibn al-Musayyab. He said, '*Respond to the Commander of the Believers.*' He (Sa'id ibn al-Musayyab) said, '*What does he need?*' He responded, '*To speak with you.*' He (Sa'id ibn al-Musayyab) said, '*I am not among those with whom he speaks.*' So, the gatekeeper returned and informed him of that.

Al-Bukhari said in his Tarikh, '*I heard Ibn Abi Iyas say, "I witnessed Hammad ibn Salamah when the Sultan summoned him. He said, 'Go to them? By Allah I do not do that.'"*' He meant he would not do it.

Al-Khatib narrated about Hammad ibn Salamah, that one of the caliphs sent a messenger to him saying, '*A matter has arisen. Can we ask you about it?*' He said to the messenger, '*We have met people who do not go to anyone because of the hadiths that have reached them. If you have a question, write it down and we will respond to you by writing.*'

Abu al-Hasan ibn Fihr narrated, in *Kitab Fada'il Malik*, that 'Abdullah ibn Rafi' and others said:

> Harun al-Rashid arrived in Madinah and sent al-Barmaki to Malik to say to him, '*Bring the book that you have written so that I may hear it from you.*' Malik responded to al-Barmaki, '*Greet him with peace and tell him that knowledge does not go to anyone. You have to go to it.*' So, al-Barmaki returned to Harun and said to him, '*O, Commander of the Believers! It will reach the people of Iraq that you have*

52

demanded something of Malik, and he has disobeyed you in it. Force him to come to you.' He replied, *'Do not be the foremost in disrespecting knowledge, such that Allah will humiliate you.'*

'Ammar said, in his *Tarikh*:

Ibn Munir narrates that the ruler of Bukhara sent a letter to Muhammad ibn Isma'il al-Bukhari that said, *'Bring your Kitab al-Jami'[9] and al-Tarikh so that I may hear them from you.'* Al-Bukhari said to the messenger, *'I do not disrespect knowledge, nor do I go to the doors of the rulers. If you need anything, then come to my mosque or my home.'*

Na'im ibn al-Hadaym said in his famous short work, that Khalaf ibn Tamim narrated, from Abu Humam al-Kala'i, that al-Hasan passed by some reciters at the door of the rulers and said, *'Have you forsaken your watering place, flattened your sandals, and come carrying knowledge upon your neck to their door? Indeed, if you had sat in your house, it would be better for you. You have separated. May Allah separate between you.'*

Al-Zajjaj relates in his Amali, that Abu Bakr ibn al-Hasan informed him that 'Abd al-Rahman ibn Akhi al-Asma'i informed him, on the authority of his uncle, that al-Hasan al-Basri passed by Abu 'Umar ibn Hubayrah. Some reciters were sitting there. He greeted them and then said:

Why are you sitting here having let your moustaches grow long, shaved your heads, shortened your sleeves, and flattened your sandals? By Allah! If you had abstained from what they possessed, they would desire what you possess. However, you have desired what they possess, so they have abstained from what you possess. You have dishonoured the reciters. May Allah dishonour you.

---

[9] *Al-Jami' al-sahih al-Bukhari*

Ibn Najjar narrated that al-Hasan said:

> Your happiness is in your safety, or your religion being
> saved. So, withhold your hands from the blood of the
> Muslims and withhold your hands from their wealth. And,
> restrain your tongues from their honour. Do not sit with
> heretical people and do not go to the rulers so that you will
> not become confused regarding your religion.

18
THREE KINDS OF SCHOLARS

ABU NA'IM NARRATED IN AL-HILYAH that Wahb ibn al-Ward said:

> It has reached us that there are three kinds of scholars: a scholar that learns for the sake of the rulers, a scholar that learns to be praised for his knowledge among the sinful, and a scholar that learns for his own sake. He does not want anything with it, he only fears that he may act without knowledge, and that the corruption caused by that would be greater than the good.

Abu Na'im narrated in *al-Hilyah* that Abu Salih al-Antaki said, '*I heard Ibn al-Mubarak say, "If someone obtains knowledge, they will be tested in one of three ways: He will either die, taking his knowledge with him, or he will forget it, or he will frequent the rulers and his knowledge will abandon him."*'

Al-Khatib al-Baghdadi narrated, regarding Malik, in a letter that he wrote to Qadi al-Ra'ishi: 'Ali ibn Sa'id informed us that Ishaq ibn Yahya said that Malik Ibn Anas ﷺ said, '*I received the following from more than ten men from among the tabi'in: Do not approach them and do not command them,*' meaning the rulers.

Ibn Bakawayhi al-Shirazi said, in *Akhbar al-Sufiyyah*, Salamah ibn Muhammad al-Takrini narrated that Muhammad ibn 'Ali al-Takrini narrated that Ya'qub ibn Ishaq informed him that 'Abdullah ibn Muhammad al-Qurayshi said:

> We were with Sufyan al-Thawri in Makkah and there came to him a letter from his children in Kufah. It said, '*Our neediness has reached the extent that we roast pebbles and eat them.*' Sufyan began to cry. Then, one of his companions said to him, '*O, Abu 'Abdullah! If you would go to the ruler,*

you would get whatever you want.' Sufyan said, 'By Allah! I do not ask for worldly goods from the One who owns them. How can I ask them of those who do not own them?'

'Abd al-Wahid narrated saying *'Ahmad ibn Muhammad Hamdun informed us that Abu 'Isa al-Anbari informed him that Ibn Mahuf informed him that 'Abdullah ibn Husayn informed him that he heard Sufyan al-Thawri say, "Show strength against the people of the world by not greeting them with peace."'*

I heard *'Abdullah ibn Abu Ja'far say that Hassan informed him that Ahmad ibn Abi al-Hawra' informed him saying, 'I said to Abu Sulayman, "The scholars dispute with one another." He became angry and said, "Do you not see that some scholars go to the doors of the rulers and take their money?"'*

'Abd al-Wahid ibn Bakr narrated to me saying:

> I heard Muhammad ibn Dawud al-Daynuri say, 'I heard Ahmad ibn al-Silt say, "A man came to Bishr ibn al-Harith and said to him, 'O, my Master! The ruler see is seeking out the pious. Do you think I should hide?' Bishr said to him, 'Get out from my presence. It is not permissible for a donkey to allure us through your mentioning him.'"'

Abu al-'Ala' informed us saying:

> I heard Ahmad ibn Muhammad al-Qushayri say, 'I heard Salih ibn Khalifah al-Karkhi say, "I heard Sufyan al-Thawri say, 'The poor among the reciters took a means towards worldly pleasure, saying, "We enter upon the rulers and relieve the distress of those who are suffering and plead for the release of those imprisoned."'"'

❀

19

THE BENEFIT OF THE PEOPLE OF KNOWLEDGE DEFENDING KNOWLEDGE

ABU 'ALI AL-AMADI SAID IN HIS TA'LIQ, 'Abu Muhammad Ja'far ibn Mus'ab ibn al-Zubayr narrated, on the authority of his grandfather al-Zubayr ibn al-Harith, "Abu al-Karam 'Uqbah ibn Mukarram ibn 'Uqbah narrated to us on the authority of Yazid ibn Kamit, that 'Ammar ibn Sayf heard Sufyan al-Thawri saying, *'Looking at the ruler is sinful.'"'*

Ibn Bakawayhi narrated that al-Fudayl ibn 'Iyad said:

> If the people of knowledge had respected themselves, if they had been avaricious of their religion, honoured knowledge, protected it, and given it the status that Allah had given it, the necks of the tyrants would bow before them. And people would follow them, busying themselves with what concerns them: the might of Islam and its people. However, they lowered themselves; they did not attain what their religion had conferred upon them, since worldly pleasures were granted to them. Thus, they were humiliated and dismissed among mankind.

Al-Amidi said:

> Abu al-'Abbas said, 'Tahir ibn 'Abdullah ibn Tahir left Khurasan for Hajj during the lifetime of his father. He stayed in the house of Ishaq ibn Ibrahim and Ishaq sent for the scholars. Ibrahim ibn Tahir came to them and taught them. Then, the people of religion and jurisprudence came. Ibn al-A'rabi and Abu Nasr, the companion of al-Asma'i, also came. He then invited for Abu 'Ubayd al-Qasim ibn Salam to come. However, he refused, maintaining that

57

knowledge should be sought. Ishaq became angry at what he had said in his letter. 'Abdullah ibn Tahir would send him (Abu 'Ubayd) one thousand dirhams. However, Ishaq cut him off and did not send it to him. He sent a letter to 'Abdullah telling him what had happened. However, 'Abdullah wrote to him, 'O, Abu al-Khayr! Regarding what you have informed us of, Abu 'Ubayd spoke the truth. And I have doubled for him his maintenance because of his action. Give him what he is owed, and after that, pay him what he deserves.'

20

ABU HAZIM AL-ZAHID AND
THE RULERS OF BANI UMAYYAH

IBN ʿASAKIR NARRATES, by way of Ibn Wahb, that ʿAbd al-Rahman ibn Yazid said:

> Abu Hazim narrated to us that Sulayman ibn Hashim ibn ʿAbd al-Malik arrived in Madinah. So, he sent for Abu Hazim who entered upon him. He said, *'I greeted him while supporting myself with my cane. He said, "Do you not speak?" I said, "I have no need to speak. I only came for the need for which you sent for me. I do not go to everyone who sends for me. If it were not for the sake of avoiding your evil, I would not have come. I was around to see the people of the world seeking the people of knowledge wherever they were, and the people of knowledge would fulfil the worldly and otherworldly needs of the people of the world. The people of this world were always in need of the people of knowledge to obtain the knowledge they needed. Then, things changed with time, and the people of knowledge began to seek out the people of this world wherever they were. Thus, both parties were afflicted with trials. The people of this world abandoned the knowledge that they adhered to, because they saw that the people of knowledge came to them. And the people of knowledge were made fat from what their followers, the people of this world, distributed to them."'*

Ibn Abi Dunya, al-Khara'iti and Ibn ʿAsakir narrated that Zam'ah ibn Salih said:

> One of the Bani Umayyah wrote to Abu Hazim, insisting that he inform him of his needs. The latter responded,

'As to what follows, I received your letter insisting that I inform you of my needs. Impossible! I have raised my needs to my Lord. I have accepted what He has given me, and I am satisfied with that which He has withheld.'

Ibn 'Asakir narrated on the authority of 'Abd al-Jabbar ibn 'Abd al-'Aziz ibn Abi Hazim, from his father, from his grandfather, that Sulayman ibn 'Abd al-Malik entered Madinah. He stayed there for three days. He said, *'Is there any person who met the Companions of Muhammad* ﷺ *that may teach us?'* It was said, *'There is a man here who is called Abu Hazim,'* so he sent for him. When he came, Sulayman said *'O, Abu Hazim! What is this slight? All the inhabitants of Madinah have come to me but you did not come.'* Abu Hazim said, *'When people are upon what is correct, the governors need the scholars, and the scholars flee with their religion from the governors.'*

Al-Bayhaqi and Ibn 'Asakir narrated that Zam'ah ibn Salih said:

Al-Zahidi said to Sulayman ibn Abi Hashim, 'Why don't you ask Abu Hazim what he said about the scholars?' He replied, 'O, Abu Hazim! What have you said about the scholars?' He said, *'Would I say anything but good about the scholars? I met the scholars and when he and his companions saw that, they learned knowledge and did not become independent through it. The people of the world became, through their worldly gods, free of need of their knowledge. When they saw that, they slandered the people of the world with their knowledge, and the people did not grant them anything from their worldly goods. He and his companions are not scholars; they are merely narrators.'*

Abu Na'im and Ibn 'Asakir narrated that Yusuf ibn Asbat said:

Someone informed me that one of the rulers sent for Abu Hazim. He came to him with an African, al-Zuhri, and others. He (the ruler) said, 'Speak, O, Abu Hazim.' He said, *'The best of the rulers are those who love the scholars, and the worst of the scholars are those who love the rulers. Among the scholars of the past were those who, when the rulers summoned them, would not go to them. And when they asked them, they did not satisfy them. Still, the rulers would come to the scholars in their houses and ask them. In that, there was a rectification of the rulers and a rectification of the scholars. When some people saw that, they said, "Why don't we seek knowledge that we may be like them." So they sought knowledge, went to the rulers, and narrated to them. Thus, the scholars corrupted the rulers, and the rulers corrupted the scholars.'*

Al-Bayhaqi narrated in *al-Zuhd*, and Ibn ʿAsakir also narrated, that Sufyan said:

Oneʿof the rulers said to Abu Hazim, 'Inform me of your needs.' He replied, *'Impossible! I have raised my needs to the One who alone can grant one's needs. I am satisfied with what He has given me, and I am satisfied with what He withheld. The scholars of the past were sought out by the ruler and fled from him, while the scholars of today sought knowledge until, when they had gathered it and put on an heir of knowledge, they came to the doors of the rulers. But the rulers flee from them while they seek them out.'*

Ibn ʿAsakir narrated that Muhammad ibn ʿAjlan al-Madini said:

Sulayman ibn Hisham sent for Abu Hazim and said to him, 'Speak'. He said, *'I have no need of speaking. If it were not to avoid your evil, I would never have come to you. A time passed upon us where the rulers would seek the scholars and seek what they possessed, and they were satisfied with it. In that, there was good for both parties. However, these days, the scholars seek out the rulers and they depend upon them. They have considered lowly what they possess. Thus, the rulers have said, "They have only sought what we possess because what we have is better than what they have." In that is corruptions for both groups.'* Sulayman ibn Hashim said, 'You have spoken the truth.'

Ibn ʿAsakir narrates by way of Abu Qalabah ʿAbd al-Malik ibn Muhammad al-Qurayshi who said, 'Abu Saʿid al-Asmaʾi narrated to us on the authority of Ibn Abi Zinad, that the latter's father said, *"All the jurists in Madinah used to come to 'Umar ibn 'Abd al-'Aziz, except Sa'id ibn al-Musayyab. 'Umar wanted to have a messenger between them. I was the messenger between them.'"*

Ibn 'Asakir narrated that al-Awza'i said:

> 'Ata' al-Khurasani went to Hisham ibn 'Abd al-Malik. He sat next to Makhul and said to him, 'Is there anyone who can move us?' In other words: is there anyone to grant them their needs? He said, 'Yes. Yazid ibn Maysarah.' So, he went to him and said, 'Give us. May Allah have mercy on you.' He said, 'Of course. May Allah have mercy on you. The scholars used to be such that whatever they learned, they put into practice. Their action caused them to be busy and their being occupied caused them to need. When they began to have needs, they sought them, and when they sought them, they would do so in secret.' He said, 'Repeat that to me', so he repeated it and returned without meeting Hisham.

21

HAMMAD IBN SALAMAH AND THE GOVERNOR OF IRAQ

AL-KHATIB AND IBN ʿASAKIR NARRATED that Muqatil ibn Salih al-Khurasani said:

I entered upon Hammad ibn Salamah and, while I was sitting with him, someone knocked on the door. He said, '*O, girl! Go out and see who it is.*' She said, '*It is the messenger of Muhammad ibn Sulayman al-Hashimi.*' He said, '*Tell him to enter alone.*' He entered, greeted him, and delivered him a letter. He said, '*Read it.*' It said, '*In the Name of Allah, the Beneficent, the Merciful. From Muhammad ibn Sulayman to Hammad ibn Salamah. To proceed: May Allah grant you, this day, the good that He has granted His awliya' and His obedient servants. A situation has arisen so I have come to ask you about it.*' He said, '*O, girl! Bring the writing utensils. Turn the letter over and write: "To proceed: May Allah also grant you, this day, that which He has granted His awliya' and His obedient servants. We saw a time when the scholars would not go to anyone. If a situation has arisen, come and ask whatever you wish. But if you come to me, come alone and do not come on horseback. Come on foot, or I will neither counsel you nor myself. Peace."*' While I was with him, someone knocked on the door again. He said, '*O, girl! Go out and see who it is.*' She said, '*It is Muhammad ibn Sulayman.*' He said, '*Tell him to enter alone.*' So, he entered and greeted him. Then, he sat before him and started by saying, '*Why is it that when I look at you, I am filled with awe?*' Hammad said, '*I heard Thabit al-Bannani say, "I heard Anas ibn Malik say, 'I heard the Messenger of*

Allah (S) say, "When knowledge is sought for Allah's sake, everything flees from it. But when it is to increase one's wealth and riches, it flees from everything.""""

Then he related the rest of the story.

Ibn al-Najjar narrated in his *Tarikh* that Ibn al-Aswad said, 'Ma'mun said, "Knowledge remained powerful until it was carried to the doors of kings and people took a wage for it. Thus, Allah removed the beauty from their hearts and prevented them from acting upon it (the knowledge).'"

22

THE SITUATION OF THOSE WHO ASSOCIATE WITH THE RULERS

AL-GHAZALI COMPOSED A CHAPTER IN AL-IHYA' on associating with the rulers, and the ruling on frequenting visitation of their circles and entering upon them. He said:

> You should know that, with the rulers, you will be in one of three states: the first is the worst of them. It is that you should enter upon them. The second, which is lighter than the first, is that they should enter upon you. The third, which is the safest, is that you should avoid them, such that you do not see them, nor do they see you.

As for the first, which is that you should enter upon them, it is very blameworthy in the Sacred Law. And it has heavy consequences that are mutawatir in traditional reports and accounts.

Sufyan said, '*In Hell, there is a valley in which only those reciters that used to visit the rulers will live.*'

Al-Awza'i said, '*Nothing is more hated to Allah than a scholar who visits a governor.*'

Wahib said, regarding those who enter upon the rulers, '*A fly on a garbage pile is better than a reciter at their door.*'

When al-Zuhri associated with the ruler, one of his brethren that were religious wrote to him:

> May Allah grant us both freedom from seditions and trials, O Abu Bakr. You have entered a situation such that it is necessary for those that know you to supplicate for you and be gentle with you. You have become an elderly sheikh. You should be filled with the blessings of Allah due to what

He granted you of understanding of His Book, and what He taught you of the Sunnah of His Prophet ﷺ. But that is not the case. Allah has taken a pact with the scholars and I know that the smallest sin that you have committed, and the lightest burden that you have carried is that you have befriended a terrible oppressor. You have opened to yourself the path of being seduced by your sins to the point that you will not support the truth nor abandon falsehood when we call your attention to it. They have taken you as a pole: the churn of their oppression turns around you. They have taken you as a bridge: they pass over you to their evil deeds. They have taken you as a ladder: they use you to rise towards their misguidance. By you, they cast doubt on the scholars and they capture, through you, the hearts of the ignorant. What is the slightest thing that they have given you in comparison with what they have taken from you? What is the greatest thing that they have taken from you? While they are corrupting your religion, you are not safe from being among those who Allah mentions the following about them: '*There succeeded them a generation that neglected the prayer and followed their false desires*' (Maryam 19:59).

You are dealing with someone who is not ignorant, and one who is not negligent is trying to preserve you. So, amend your religion for you have entered sickness into it, and prepare your provisions, for a long journey has drawn near to you. Nothing in the Earth or the Heavens is hidden from Allah. Peace.

All these traditions and reports indicate the sedition and the kinds of corruption that accompany sitting with the rulers. However, we will give a juristic explanation, distinguishing between what is illicit, what is disliked, and what is permissible with regard to that. We say: **If someone enters upon the ruler, he exposes himself to disobedience of Allah, either in action, his silence, his words, or his belief. These are four matters no one is safe from.** As for the action, it is because the majority of situations in which someone enters upon them will be in stolen or confiscated property. And entering property without permission from its owner is illicit.

Also, it is not permissible to humble oneself before an oppressor, except solely to save one's life. As for kissing his hand or kneeling on one's knees in servitude, it is illicit. In fact, some of the predecessors had gone to such lengths as to prohibit returning their greeting of peace. They prescribed that one should turn away from them in contempt for the gathering of those near them or sitting on their carpets, since most of their wealth is illicit.

As for your silence, one would see in in their gatherings things such as silk sheets, silver utensils, and silk clothing. Further, most of them wear clothing that is illicit. Anyone who sees an evil deed and remains silent regarding it, he will have a share in that evil deed. One would also hear, from their speech, that which is lewd or abominable. Or, they may abuse people or curse them, and remaining silent about any of that is unlawful.

One may say, '*He may fear for himself. In that case, he would be excused for remaining silent.*' That is true. However, he had no need to expose himself to that which is not permissible. He is not excused for that because, had he not entered, he would not have witnessed anything. Therefore, he would not have been subject to responsibility. So, the excuse is removed from him. In addition, if someone knows that a place is full of corruption, and that he is unable to remove it, it is not permissible for him to be in that place such that these activities would take place in front of him, and he would witness them and remain silent. Rather, he would try not to witness them.

Perhaps one would say, '*That only applies to someone who supplicates for the oppressor, praises him, affirms what is patently false in his words, disputes with you in front of him, tries to flatter him to his face, manifests love or allegiance to him, but not to one who merely desires to meet him.*' That desire to meet him includes all those situations and times, because, in most cases, it [the meeting] is not restricted to greetings. Rather, one usually stays and speaks instead of leaving. In all these different kinds of speech, there is supplication which is not permissible for him except if he should say, '*May Allah rectify you*' or, '*May Allah enable you to do good*' or, '*May Allah prolong your life*' or other similar supplications. As for supplicating for protection, prolonged reign, being covered in blessings, or speaking of the Lord, none of that is permissible.

The Prophet ﷺ, '*If someone supplicates for the long life of the oppressor, he has desired for Allah ﷻ to be disobeyed in His Earth.*' If such a supplication should cross the limit into praise, by mentioning characteristics that he does not possess, he will either be a liar, a hypocrite, or honouring an oppressor. And all three of those are sins. He ﷺ said, '*Allah becomes angry when a transgressor is praised.*' In another report, he said, '*If someone honours a transgressor, he has assisted in the destruction of Islam.*'

Suppose that should cross the limits into affirmation, assistance, and commendation, this assistance and praise amount to supporting him in sin and increase his desire for that sin. Likewise, condemnation, criticism, and rebuke of it are deterrents and weaken the sin's allures. And assisting someone in sin is itself a sin, even if one does so with a single word. Sufyan was asked regarding an oppressor who was close to perishing in a desert, '*Should someone give him to drink?*' He said, '*No. Pray that he dies. For that is you helping him.*'

Also, he will not be safe from corruption seeping into his heart. He will look at the ruler's having ample blessings and begin to look down upon the blessing of Allah ﷻ upon him. Therefore, he will be incurring what the Messenger of Allah ﷺ forbade when he said, '*O, muhajirun! Do not enter upon the people of this world for it causes you to reject [your allotted] sustenance.*' In addition, this includes the danger of others following him in entering upon them [the people of this world]. Furthermore, that is part of the compounding of his sin. Moreover, it makes it attractive for others if he is among those who are followed in their actions. And all of that is disliked, if not prohibited entirely.

It is therefore impermissible to enter upon them, except with **two excuses.** The first is as a result of them forcing him, such that his following the order would be by force and not by honour, knowing that if he were to deny it, he would be entered by force. The second is that he enters upon them to prevent them from oppressing a Muslim. That is a dispensation for him with the condition that he does not lie, and that he does not leave out any advice that must be said.

If you were to say, '*The scholars of the salaf entered upon the ruler*,' I would say, 'Yes. *Learn the way they entered and then enter.*' It has been narrated that Hisham ibn 'Abd al-Malik went to Hajj in Makkah. When he entered, he said, '*Bring me a man from the Companions.*' It was said, '*O, Commander of the Believers! They have all perished.*' He said, '*Then from the tabi'in*', so Tawus al-Yamani was brought. When he entered upon him, he took off his sandals at the margins of his carpet. He did not greet the advisers of the Commander of the Believers. However, he said, '*Peace be upon you, O, Hisham!*' And he did not call him by his title. He sat on his garment and he said, '*How are you O, Hisham?*' So, Hisham became very angry until he intended to kill him. He said, '*What has caused you to do what you have done?*' He (Tawus) said, '*What have I done?*' His anger increased and became deeper. He said, '*You took your sandals off on the margins of my carpet, you did not kiss my hand, and you did not greet the advisers of the Commander of the Believers. You did not call me by my title, you sat on my garment without permission, and you said, "How are you, O, Hisham?"*' He replied:

> As for your words that I took off my sandals on the margins of your carpet, I take them off before the Lord of Might five times every day and he does not become angry or chastise me. As for your words that I did not kiss your hand, I heard 'Ali ibn Abi Talib ﷺ say, '*It is not permissible for a man to kiss the hand of anyone except his wife, with desire, or his children, out of mercy.*' As for your words, 'You did not greet my advisers', not all people are pleased with your advisers, so I hated to lie. As for your words that I did not call you by your title, Allah ﷻ called His *awliya'* saying 'O, Adam!', 'O, Yahya,' and He called his enemies by their titles: '*Perish the hands of Abu Lahab*'. As for your words that I sat on

your garment, I heard 'Ali ibn Abi Talib saying, '*If you want to see a man of the People of the fire, look at a man who is sitting while the people around him are standing.*'

Hisham said, '*Exhort me.*' He said, '*I heard 'Ali ibn Abi Talib say, "Indeed, in Hell, there are snakes as big as camels and scorpions as big as donkeys. They will bite every ruler who is not just to his people*", then he got up and left.

Sufyan al-Thawri said:

I entered upon Abu Ja'far and he said to me, '*Inform me of your needs.*' I said to him, '*Fear Allah. You have filled the earth with injustice and oppression.*' He lowered his head and then raised it. He said, '*Inform us of your needs.*' I said, '*This house was established with the swords of the muhajirin and Ansar. They are dying of hunger, so fear Allah and give them their rights.*' He lowered his head and then raised it, and he said, '*Inform us of your needs.*' I said, "*'Umar ibn al-Khattab ؓ performed Hajj and his treasurer asked him, "How much did you spend?" He said, "I spent a little over ten dirhams." Do you see all this wealth that camels could hardly carry?*' And I left.

In the *Amali* of Sheikh Ibn 'Abd al-Salam, on which Sheikh Shihab al-Din al-Qarafi, one of the Maliki Imams, wrote a commentary, among what he (Sheikh 'Izz al-Din) said was, '*I will not be an intercessor before the Lord of the worlds and among his creation, frequenting the doors of these people.*' Al-Qarafi said, '*He ؒ was indicating that the writer [of Islamic Sciences] becomes as one who is transmitting from Allah to His servants. Thus, he is a representative of Messengerhood. And if someone is honoured with that, such a thing is ugly for him to do.*'

❀

23
THAT WHICH IS
UNBECOMING OF THE SCHOLAR

IBN AL-HAJJ said in *al-Madkhal*:

It is important, nay imperative, that the scholar does not
frequent the door of anyone among the people of the world,
because the scholar should be as the ruler at his door, not
the opposite. The truth is that he has no excuse for being
at their door, by saying that he fears an enemy or envier, or
other people who may confuse him. Or, that he hopes that
one of them will help him ward off something that he fears,
or that he hopes to fulfil the needs of the Muslims through
that, such as causing benefit or removing harm. That is not
a beneficial excuse.

As for the first, it is because if he takes that as benefit
for himself, he will not be blessed in it. Even if he does
fear what he mentioned, that is a personal benefit. And
it may bring about a situation where someone is set loose
upon him who will dispute with him over knowledge as
an expedited punishment. As for the second excuse, such a
person would be incurring a prohibited matter for the sake
of a prohibited matter whose occurrence is hypothetical
and supposed in the future. It may happen or it may not,
whereas the obligation of the moment is to refrain from
committing that act which is blameworthy according to
Sacred Law. In fact, assisting in fulfilling his own needs,
and the needs of the Muslims, requires cutting off from
the doors of the rulers, complete reliance on Allah ﷻ, and
returning to Him. For He ﷻ is the One who truly fulfils
needs, wards off fears and subjects hearts, turning them
towards whomever He wills in whichever way He wills.

He ﷺ said, addressing the Master of Creation, '*If you had spent the entire earth, you would never be able to join between people's hearts. Rather, Allah will join them*' (al-Anfal 8:63).

He ﷺ mentioned this, rejecting that anyone should have any favour over the Prophet ﷺ. And since the scholar would be following him ﷺ, he should resemble him in his reliance upon his Lord and dependence upon Him to the exclusion of all created beings. For He ﷻ will treat him with the same gentle treatment with which He treated His Prophet ﷺ. And that will save him from having to frequent the doors of the worldly people, as some people do, which is a deadly poison. If only they had restricted themselves to the previously mentioned things. However, they plunge into that which is more shameful and more severe. They say, '*Our frequenting their door is part of humility*', or from their attempts to guide them to that which is better, and other evidences they give. That causes the calamity to become complete, and if they believe that, then there is little hope that they will repent and return.

One of our scholars has transmitted that when a just person frequents the door of the judge, it would be a deficiency in his case, which would in turn cause his testimony to be rejected. If that is the case of one who frequents the door of the judge, and he is one of the scholars of the Muslims whose gathering is safe from the things that occur in the gatherings of the rulers, then how about frequenting other people? It is from a more important category, and it is more imperative to prohibit it.

In another place he said:

It is imperative that the scholar, after he has finished his formal studies, does not abandon his effort. Nor should he become bored or angry, because Allah may remove from him something that he knew in order to test his sincerity and action. His sustenance is guaranteed and it is not restricted to one place or another. He ﷺ said, '*Whoever studies knowledge, Allah will guarantee his sustenance.*'

The meaning is that He will facilitate it for him without exhaustion or difficulty, even if Allah has guaranteed the sustenance of all creation. However, the wisdom in his electing the scholar for a special mention is that it will be facilitated for him without exhaustion or difficulty. He placed his portion of exhaustion and difficulty in his lessons, readings, intent to understand, and recitation of the texts. That is from Allah ﷻ by way of gentleness and grace towards him. And that is from the *karamat* of the scholars, just as the *awliya'* have *karamat* in other, innumerable ways, such as walking on water and flying through the air.

It is imperative that he protects that noble rank from distractions such as seeking payment for teaching the Islamic sciences, speaking about them, or spreading knowledge. Someone who I trust narrated to me that he saw some of the later scholars. They were studying in college, and when they finished their studies, they said to the teacher, *'Perhaps you should walk'* because were among the children of the world. They meant that they intended to gather worldly goods through teaching knowledge. He said, *'I shy before my Lord ('azza wa jall) that these white hairs should lie in His Presence.'* They said to him, *'How is that?'* He said, *'Every morning, I say, "O, Allah! There is no one who can prevent what You have given. Nor is there anyone who can give what You have withheld." Should I say that and then stand before a created being asking him?'*

Of all people, it is most important for the scholar to trust in his Lord (*'azza wa jall*), in His giving and withholding. He has no excuse to seek payment, because if he abandons this, seeking this noble station, Allah, the Most Generous, will not put his objective to waste. He will open for him, from His unseen realm, what is better than it. And He will help him and fortify his moral constitution upon what He wills and however He wills.

Sustenance is not restricted to a single manner. The perpetual custom of Allah ﷻ is to provide for the one in that state, without him having to go to any door or seek a known means. This is because Allah wants the scholars to be isolated for Him and completely dependent upon Him in all their affairs. They should not look towards means. Rather, they should focus on the Creator and Controller of means, and the One who has complete power over them. How could a scholar not be like that when he is the guide of people and the one who clarifies the straight path which travels towards Him ﷺ. And whoever leaves things for Allah ﷻ, Allah will grant him better than it, from where he does not expect.

In the biography of ʿAli ibn al-Hasan al-Sandali in *Tabaqat al-Hanafiyyah*, it says that the ruler Malik Shah said to a scholar, '*Why do you not come to me?*' He said, '*I wanted you to be among the best of rulers through your visitation of the scholars. And I do not want to be among the worst scholars through my visitation of the rulers.*'

Ibn ʿAdi said in al-Kamil:

> I heard Abu al-Husayn Muhammad b. Muzaffar say, "I heard our Shaykhs in Egypt recognizing Abu ʿAbd al-Rahman as one of the preeminent Imams. They would describe him as someone who put much effort into his worship during the day and night. His constant effort was because, one day, he abandoned a lunch with the governor of Egypt. So, people began to describe him as gallant, upholding the transmitted Sunnah and avoiding the gathering of the ruler whom he had avoided. So, that became his practice until he was martyred. In *Tahdhib al-Kamal* of al-Muzani, in the biography of Abu Yahya Ahmad ibn ʿAbd al-Malik al-Harani, the sheikh of al-Bukhari, it says: Abu al-Hasan al-Maymuni said: I asked Ahmad ibn Hanbal about him (Abu Yahya) and he said, "He used to come to our gatherings. I found him to be intelligent and I did not see anything bad in him. And I found that he would easily memorize hadiths. I only saw good of him." I said to him, "I have seen a group that considers praising him blameworthy." He said, "He would frequent the ruler because of a property he owned."

⁂

24

THE MOST NOBLE THING IN THE END TIMES

IN TAHDHIB AL-KAMAL, it also says, with the author's chain of transmission from Rushdayn ibn Sa'd, who said, '*I heard Ibrahim ibn Adham say, "The most noble of things in the end times are three: A brother whose company one may keep for the sake of Allah; earning lawful income; and a word of truth in the presence of the ruler."*'

25

THE WORDS OF SOME POETS ON COMING TO THE RULERS

KHALAF IBN TAMIM SAID, 'I heard Ibrahim ibn Adham reciting the following verses':

> *I see that people only attain contentment through religion,*
> *I do not believe they can be satisfied with anything else in life.*

Al-Shashi said in his *Amali*, 'Abu al-Ghayyat narrated that Abu Bakr al-Anbari narrated to him, that his father narrated to him, "Sulayman al-Mahlabi sent one thousand dirhams to al-Khalil ibn Ahmad and requested his company. So, he returned to him one hundred thousand, and he wrote some couplets to him." It is said that the meaning of those lines was:

> *Convey to Sulayman that I am, without him, in ampleness,*
> *And in richness. However, I am not a possessor of wealth,*

> *My soul is satisfied because I don't believe that anyone,*
> *Dies through being mocked. Nor is any state permanent,*

> *For sustenance is determined and no incapacity can decrease it,*
> *Nor does any might or power increase one in it,*

> *True poverty is in the soul, not in wealth. Recognize that,*
> *Similarly, wealth is in the soul, not in possessions.*

Abu Na'im narrated in *al-Hilyah* that Muhammad ibn Wahb ibn Hisham said, 'One of our companions recited the following to Ibn al-Mubarak':

Eat al-Jarush,
Rice and flat bread,

And make sure it is lawful,
You will be saved from the heat of Hell.

And avoid as much as you are able, May Allah,
Guide you, the door of the governor.

Abu Na'im narrated in *al-Hilyah* that Ahmad ibn Hanbal al-Maruzi said, 'It was said to 'Abdullah ibn al-Mubarak, "Isma'il ibn 'Aliyyah has taken control of the charity." So, Ibn al-Mubarak wrote to him with some poetry of the following meaning:

O, you who has made knowledge into a falcon,
Hunting the wealth of the poor,

Taking the worldly goods for its own self,
With a fraud that destroys the religion,

Where are the traditions you used to narrate,
From Ibn 'Awf and Ibn Sirin,

If you say you were forced, how is it that.
The donkey of knowledge has slipped in the mud.

When he read the letter, he cried and repented.[10]

---

[10] Four additional poems were not included in this translation at the discretion of the translator.

Here ends the Imam's work concerning 'What the Distinguished Experts Have Narrated Regarding Never Visiting the Rulers'. And all praise is due to Allah, Lord of all the worlds. May blessings and peace be upon the Master of the Messengers, our Master Muhammad, his family and his companions.

www.ingramcontent.com/pod-product-compliance
Lightning Source LLC
Chambersburg PA
CBHW030349100526
44592CB00010B/889